JUSTICE

To my Dominican sisters who have challenged me
for more than thirty years
"to reclaim [my] passion for contemplation,"
"to hold the promotion of justice as a singular priority,"
"and to study, live, and teach the mysteries of the universe
and the sacredness of all creation."

*From the "Foreword" of the
Constitutions of the Sisters of St. Dominic,
Caldwell, N.J.*

JUSTICE
A Biblical Perspective

Carol J. Dempsey

CHALICE
PRESS
ST. LOUIS, MISSOURI

Copyright © 2008 by Carol J. Dempsey

All rights reserved. For permission to reuse content, please contact Copyright Clearance Center, www.copyright.com, 222 Rosewood Drive, Danvers, MA 01923, (978) 750-8400.

Bible quotations, unless otherwise noted, are from the *New Revised Standard Version Bible,* copyright 1989, Division of Christian Education of the National Council of the Churches of Christ in the United States of America. Used by permission. All rights reserved.

Cover image: Elizabeth Wright, using photographs from Digital Vision/GettyImages and Comstock
Cover and interior design: Elizabeth Wright

BS
680
.J8
D46
2008

Visit Chalice Press on the World Wide Web at
www.chalicepress.com

10 9 8 7 6 5 4 3 2 1   08 09 10 11 12

Library of Congress Cataloging–in–Publication Data

Dempsey, Carol J.
  Justice: A biblical perspective / Carol J. Dempsey.
     p. cm.
  ISBN 978-0-8272-1718-8
  1. Justice—Biblical teaching. I. Title.
  BS680.J8D46 2008
  241'.662—dc22
                                            2007046279

Printed in the United States of America

Contents

Acknowledgments	vii
Introduction	1
1. Justice and Liberation Attained through Violence	9
2. Hospitality of Heart	45
3. Women, Children, Slaves, and Donkeys	63
4. Compassion	87
5. Peace	101
Epilogue	111
Notes	115
Select Bibliography	121
Biblical Index	125
Index of Authors and Terms	133

Acknowledgments

Few books are written without the support and encouragement of wonderful people whose spirit is contained within the pages of the text. This book on justice is no different, and it has taken several years to see the light of day. Research and work on the manuscript began in late 1999 and came to an abrupt halt when my brother George, the father of five young children, suffered a brain aneurysm, and the prognosis was bad. By the sheer grace of God, he eventually made a full recovery. Work then continued on the manuscript, passing from the hands of Jon Berquist to Jane McAvoy, who encouraged my work with great enthusiasm. Jane passed away unexpectedly, and then work continued with Trent Butler, who has kept my hand to the page. To Jon, the memory of Jane, and Trent, I am grateful for their faithfulness to this project. To my colleagues at Chalice Press, I also owe a great debt of gratitude for their kindness and generous spirit, especially former Chalice Press staffers Sarah Tasic and Susie Burgess. I owe a special debt of gratitude to Pablo Jiménez, editor; Gail Stobaugh, copy editor; Lisa Scronce, publishing assistant; and Elizabeth Wright, art director.

I would be remiss if I did not express my gratitude to my family, friends, and colleagues, especially Bill Bellinger of Baylor University, whose conversations about justice through our work together at the College Theology Society have helped me shape my thoughts. To Aric Ward, a former graduate student in theology who helped to prepare part of this manuscript, I express my heartfelt thanks. I also wish to thank the University of Portland for supporting my research through the Arthur

Butine Faculty Development Fund. I am especially grateful to the university's library staff—Drew Harrington, Caroline Mann, Vickie Hamilton, Heidi Senior, Diane Sotak, and Stephanie Michel. Finally, I am thankful to Holly, Joel, Kira, and Joelene, my zebra finch family, and Katie Rose and Kelli Mae, parrotlets, whose peeps and playfulness kept my wonder alive.

January 6, 2008
Feast of the Epiphany

INTRODUCTION

Justice

A Divine Imperative—
A Contemporary Challenge

Thousands of years ago, in a time different and yet not so different from our own, an ancient poet named Isaiah proclaimed these timeless prophetic words in a prayer to his God:

> Therefore justice is far from us,
>   and righteousness does not reach us;
> we wait for light and lo! There is darkness;
>   and for brightness, but we walk in gloom.
> We grope like the blind along a wall,
>   groping like those who have no eyes;
> we stumble at noon as in the twilight,
>   among the vigorous as though we were dead.
> We all growl like bears;
>   like doves we moan mournfully.

2 Justice

> We wait for justice, but there is none;
>   for salvation, but it is far from us.
> For our transgressions before you are many,
>   and our sins testify against us.
> Our transgressions indeed are with us,
>   and we know our iniquities:
> transgressing, and denying the Lord,
>   and turning away from following our God,
> talking oppression and revolt,
>   conceiving lying words and uttering them from the heart.
> Justice is turned back,
>   and righteousness stands at a distance;
> for truth stumbles in the public square,
>   and uprightness cannot enter.
> Truth is lacking,
>   and whoever turns from evil is despoiled.
>   (Isa. 59:9–15)

The ancient Israelite community struggled among themselves because some of their members got caught in the endless web of greed, violence, and the abuse of power that causes a myriad of injustices, leaving the most vulnerable with few alternatives except to succumb to those more powerful than themselves. Clearly the root cause of injustice within the Israelite community was the loss of "right relationship"—right relationship with their God and, consequently, right relationship with one another.[1]

Despite the depravity that existed within the social world of Israel, there was, however, always a sense of hope and the presence of the Divine embodied in other poets from within the community. These poets continually spoke out against injustice and called the people back to a vision of justice, righteousness, and loving-kindness. One such example was Micah, who, as a representative member of the Israelite community, interceded with God on Israel's behalf. Aware of his people's transgressions,[2] this contrite poet posed a most poignant yet bewildered question to his God:

> With what shall I come before the LORD,
>   and bow myself before God on high?
> Shall I come before him with burn offerings,
>   with calves a year old?
> Will the LORD be pleased with thousands of rams,
>   with ten thousands of rivers of oil?
> Shall I give my firstborn for my transgression,
>   the fruit of my body for the sin of my soul?
>   (Mic. 6:6–7)

The divine response that Micah receives is gentle and just as poignant:

> He has told you, O mortal, what is good;
>   and what does the LORD require of you
> but to do justice, and to love kindness,
>   and to walk humbly with your God?
>   (Mic. 6:8)

"To do justice," "to love kindness," and "to walk humbly with your God": this message was a word of instruction not just to Micah but also to the perpetrators of injustice as well as to the victims of injustice. Israel was called, as an entire community, "to act justly," "to love kindness," and "to walk humbly with [their] God."

Justice and loving-kindness, accompanied by a humble walk with God, was at the heart of Israel's life as a community of faith, a people whom God chose not because they were more numerous than any other people, and not because they were the fewest of all peoples. According to the book of Deuteronomy, God chose the Israelite people because God loved them.[3]

The theme of justice, one of the main themes of the Old Testament and Jewish tradition,[4] is also central to the New Testament and the Christian tradition. For example, in Matthew's gospel, the writer portrays Jesus upbraiding the scribes and

4 *Justice*

Pharisees because they have neglected "the weightier matters of the law: justice and mercy and faith" (Mt. 23:23).[5] One of the most exquisite examples of justice in the New Testament, however, is found in the crucifixion narrative as described by the writer of Luke's gospel (see Lk. 23:26–43), who portrays Jesus extending mercy to his persecutors and enemies: "Then Jesus said, 'Father forgive them; for they do not know what they are doing'" (v. 34). To those witnessing Jesus' crucifixion—both friends and foes—these words would have sounded foolish. And yet, paradoxically, these words of reconciliation could be understood as an expression of justice at its deepest level—justice that gives way to compassion toward those guilty of injustice who, for some reason, do not truly understand what they are doing or have done to another or others.[6]

This understanding of justice illumines Matthew 12:18–21, a passage based on Isaiah, that can be understood as Jesus' inaugural vision of his vocation:

> Here is my servant, whom I have chosen,
>   my beloved, with whom my soul is well pleased.
> I will put my Spirit upon him,
>   and he will proclaim justice to the Gentiles.
> He will not wrangle or cry aloud,
>   nor will anyone hear his voice in the streets.
> He will not break a bruised reed
>   or quench a smoldering wick
> until he brings justice to victory.
>   And in his name the Gentiles will hope.
>   (vv. 18–21)

In light of the entire gospel message of Matthew and Jesus' way of life, a "bruised reed" and "a smoldering wick" could infer not only the one suffering injustice but also the one causing it. Justice will be proclaimed to the Gentiles and to everyone else as well.[7]

Thus both the Old and New Testaments attest that justice was more than a virtue. For the people of Israel and for Jesus and his followers, justice was a divine imperative.[8] For the community of believers today, justice continues to be both a divine imperative and a contemporary challenge.

In this twenty-first century, the human community grapples with many of the same struggles as did the peoples of the ancient world, and always the search for justice hangs in the balance. This book looks at the topic of justice in relation to the biblical text to discover how the text's description of justice reflects the historical, social, and cultural situation of its day on the one hand, and how it transcends its times on the other to provide contemporary readers and listeners with a hopeful, eschatological vision of justice for all creation. This vision, which has already begun to unfold in our midst, has a transformative potential for all of life. Furthermore, the vision is hastened every time a sword is beaten into a plowshare or a spear into a pruning hook as nations strive to work at peace instead of taking up arms to settle differences, as the poet Isaiah so eloquently expressed in his eschatological vision that remains prophetic for today (see Isa. 2:2–4).

Unlike other volumes on biblical justice,[9] this volume proceeds from a thematic and reader-centered approach and is informed by contemporary social, ideological, and ecological concerns. Texts are chosen in relation to themes being developed and serve as case studies to be explored and pondered again and again. This work is intended not only for scholars and students but also, and most especially, for a wider, more general audience. In addition to the introduction, the volume consists of five chapters and an epilogue. Each chapter contains an analysis of selected biblical texts that support and develop each chapter's theme. The Introduction provides an overview of the volume as a whole, and sets the stage for what is to follow.

Chapter 1 focuses on the world of the Old Testament and discusses the social location, worldview, and religious and cultural situation of the ancient Israelite people. The chapter explores such concepts as *lex talionis* and the deuteronomistic theology of retribution. The chapter also highlights such points as the ancient people's understanding of divine retribution, justice that was primitive, and metaphorical language for God as judge and divine warrior. These points are developed through a study of selected passages chosen from the Old Testament. Included in this chapter also are various passages selected from the New Testament that give another view of justice. These passages exemplify the implementation of justice through verbal confrontation, parables, verbal condemnation, and an emphasis on compassion for one's enemies. Hence, the chapter presents a contrast between how justice was sometimes carried out in the Old Testament, and how it was carried out in the teachings of the New Testament.

Caution needs to be exercised on the part of the reader when evaluating divine justice in the Bible in general and in the Old Testament in particular. The biblical text as a whole is the product of many layers of editing and redaction. It is also the compilation of the many theological perspectives of its authors and later editors, all of whom have been influenced by the cultures of their day. Thus the image of an all-powerful, sovereign, warrior-God who controls history, its outcome of events, and the destiny of a people—as the prophets sometimes depict—reflects a royal theology. This theology was consistent with the time of Israel's monarchy when kings were viewed as "gods" and supreme rulers in the land. The exercise of their power was oftentimes more in keeping with domination than dominion. Thus, the understanding and interpretation of God's justice as punitive often mirrors the culture, politics, laws, and problems of the day.

Chapter 2 explores the theme of "hospitality of heart" as the spirit of justice. The chapter begins with a focus on the intrinsic goodness of all creation, and God's care for all of creation. This chapter emphasizes the need for the development of a new ethic of socio-ecological justice that expresses concern for the well being of all creation. The second part of the chapter then moves to an emphasis on social justice, inclusive of one's enemies. The third part focuses on justice to the stranger and slave.

Chapter 3 looks at the concept of and need for justice in relation to particular groups of characters in the Bible—namely, women, children, servants/slaves, and animals. Links are made between human and nonhuman suffering and the need for justice for all creation.

Chapter 4 focuses on compassion and is divided into four sections. The first section highlights the role that compassion plays in relation to justice and transgression. The second section considers justice and compassion in relation to God's care for both human and nonhuman life—all creation. It also discusses the call for people to care for one another, regardless of whether or not a person has a relationship with that other person. Here the notion of justice is linked to a new understanding of love and vice versa. The third section emphasizes the role of compassion in the life and ministry of Jesus. Here, justice is linked to compassion—providing for others in their need, not because of duty but because of the shared relationship among human beings. Justice and compassion are then linked to liberation: freeing people from their suffering, pain, and need.

The theme of chapter 5 is "peace." This chapter gives consideration to the importance of justice in relation to being in right relationship with God, which, in turn, leads to being in right relationship with all creation. The chapter examines selected biblical texts that suggest a connection between the notion of "right relationship" and the flowering of peace. It looks at the understanding of what it means to be a "leader," and the role that justice and righteousness play in establishing harmonious relationships among all creation. Central to the discussion is the point that such harmony has peace as its fruit and the freedom for all creation to live in that peace. Lastly, the chapter looks at power and leadership, and the idea of service in relation to the person and mission of Jesus.

Finally, the Epilogue offers a series of summary remarks as well as some reflections. The call for justice remains ever-constant, the need ever-present, and the invitation ever-extended. Justice is not only a virtue and a demand but also the prophetic vocation to which all are called.

Central to the discussion of a number of biblical texts held up for critical reflection in this volume is the multifaceted way that God is portrayed by the biblical texts themselves, especially by the Old Testament texts. Readers of this work and the Bible are encouraged to remember that the biblical texts have gone through an extensive oral and written transmission process. Thus, what one sees and hears in the Bible is not God's actual voice. Rather, it is that of authors, redactors, and final editors who have tried throughout time and history to communicate something of their experience of God in relationship to the historical, cultural, social, and religious times about which they are writing. Thus, the entire biblical text is one that is theologically, historically, culturally, and socially conditioned, and it is both time-bound and timeless.

Thus, this volume recognizes that justice not only is at the heart of the biblical message and tradition but also is a way of life and a divine and human imperative that demands a response in the wake of the suffering of the entire planet. Such suffering continues to alert the human community of the urgent need for a new ethical praxis, one that will deal with the social and ecological injustices being endured by both human and nonhuman life forms. Such suffering and such a challenge are daunting, and one wonders if indeed it is too late even though the Spirit of the Holy One—the breath of life—is in the midst of all, forever transforming, forever recreating and forever renewing the face of the earth. But the faces of children, the spawning of salmon, and the delicate blossom on the twig remind us otherwise. Indeed hope does spring eternal. But hope is something we must now do as an ethical practice, and justice is something we must now embrace in every aspect of life.

Finally, this volume raises questions, tries to offer a vision, and invites readers everywhere to pick up a hoe, till and care for the earth, plant new seeds of justice in dry yet still fertile soil, and never forget that the dance of life is a dance intended for all creation.

CHAPTER 1

Justice and Liberation Attained through Violence

*An Ancient Reality—
A Contemporary Dilemma*

In the ancient world, the principle of *lex talionis* and a belief in the deuteronomistic theology of retribution influenced the Israelites' concept of justice. *Lex talionis,* also known as the law of retaliation, was popular among ancient Near Eastern cultures. Some examples of this principle are found in the Law Code of Hammurabi. Essentially, *lex talionis* advocated "an eye for an eye, and a tooth for a tooth" mentality.[1] This notion of inflicting the same kind of punishment on one another became central to the Israelite community's understanding of justice.

The deuteronomistic theology of retribution was a theological construct best described by Deuteronomy 28, which puts forth the notion of divine blessings and curses. If one were "obedient" to God and God's ways, then God would bless that person. If, however, one were disobedient, then God would curse that person. Hence, divine justice took on the characteristic of being punitive. Thus, many of the Old Testament texts that are concerned with justice reflect an expression of justice consistent with the ideas of *lex talionis* and the deuteronomistic theology of retribution.

Perhaps the most graphic examples of punitive justice, particularly as it is ascribed to God by the biblical writers and editors, is found in the texts of the prophets, beginning with those of the eighth century B.C.E., one of the most violent periods in Israel's history. These biblical texts depict Israel's prophets as solitary figures, committed deeply to their God and to their people. Repeatedly, they call their community members to repentance,[2] and warn them of the forthcoming, inevitable military invasions. The prophets perceived these horrific events as Israel's "just deserts" from God because some of the Israelites had forgotten God and God's ways, and consequently had caused others of their community to experience political, social, economic, and religious injustices. Thus, readers meet in the biblical text a God who is depicted as exercising justice punitively. For example, in Micah 2:1–3, one hears:

> Alas for those who devise wickedness
> and evil deeds on their beds!
> When morning dawns, they perform it,
> because it is in their power.
> They covet fields, and seize them;
> houses, and take them away;
> they oppress householder and house,
> people and their inheritance.
> Therefore thus says the Lord:
> Now I am devising against this family an evil
> from which you cannot remove your necks;
> and you shall not walk haughtily,
> for it will be an evil time.

Overtones of *lex talionis* and the deuteronomistic theology of retribution resound in these verses.[3]

The prophets also warned the other nations of their fates as well. Their self-serving interests had resulted in multitudinous injustices, especially those launched against Israel.[4] Jeremiah 50:13, 17–18 is a classic example:

> Because of the wrath of the LORD she [Babylon] shall not be inhabited,
>   but shall be an utter desolation;
> everyone who passes by Babylon shall be appalled
>   and hiss because of all her wounds.
>
> Israel is a hunted sheep driven away by lions. First the king of Assyria devoured it, and now at the end King Nebuchadnezzar of Babylon has gnawed its bones.

Here Jeremiah announces what is to befall Babylon because of the empire's hostility toward Israel, a nation and people special to God.[5]

Not all Old Testament texts, however, present divine justice as punitive. Various narratives contained in Genesis 3—11 portray God acting justly with compassion. One example is Genesis 4:1–16. In this narrative, Cain murders his brother, Abel (v. 8). Justice begins when God confronts Cain unassumingly and with a rhetorical question (v. 9a). Cain's response evades the truth and indicates his inability to take responsibility for the horrendous deed that he did (v. 9b). God confronts Cain a second time, indicts him, and then chastises him: Cain is now cursed (vv. 10–12). Cain, in turn, expresses to God his despair over his chastisement, and God responds with a sense of compassion. A mark on Cain's forehead will spare him his life (vv. 13–16). To be noted is that Cain does not suffer *lex talionis* either at the hands of others or at the hand of God. Furthermore, the story indicates to readers that God's exercise of justice does not follow the ways set down by human beings and the culture of the day. If it did, then Cain would have received what would have been his "just deserts"—physical death for the taking of his brother's physical life. Instead, Cain is confronted, held accountable, chastised, and made to bear the burden of his crime, but his life is spared.

Elsewhere in the Old Testament is a teaching on what has been called "the great commandment" (see Deut. 6:1–9), and a lesson on the essence of the law (see Deut. 10:12—20). Together, these two passages have become part of what has been termed the deuteronomic theology of love. This theology, exemplified in Genesis 4:1–16, seems to be what undergirds Jesus' life and mission in the New Testament. This mission culminates with Luke's portrayal of Jesus hanging on the cross and uttering the words, "Father, forgive them; for they do not know what they are doing" (Lk. 23:34). From the gospels' accounts, Jesus' justice, like God's in Genesis 4:1–16, appears to encompass concern for the transgressor, and his teaching on the love that one must have for one's enemies seems to reverse the deuteronomistic theology of retribution (see Lk. 6:27–31). Additionally, the teaching on the greatest commandment in the law, found in Matthew 22:34–40, clearly coincides with the notion of the deuteronomic theology of love. It also sheds further light on the deuteronomistic theology of retribution as a theological construct not embraced by Jesus and one that runs counter to Luke 6:27–31. The final phrase in Matthew 22:34–40, "On these two commandments hang all the law and the prophets" (v. 40), informs one's understanding of the Old Testament justice as seen in the Torah and the Prophets, both of which reflect a theology of justice that is compassionate on the one hand (Gen. 4:1–16; Hos. 11:9; Mic. 7:18–20), and punitive on the other (Ex. 21:12–25; 34:6–7; Nah. 1:2-3; Zeph. 1:2–6).

Having explored the concepts of *lex talionis* and the deuteronomistic theology of retribution as they are understood in both the Old and New Testaments and in relation to the exercise of justice as reflected in both canons, it is time to look at selected passages from the Old and New Testament, as well as from the book of Judith in the Apocrypha, to explore these themes further, while holding up the passages' content for ongoing critical theological reflection.

Exodus 7:14—12:42: The Plague Tradition

In the ancient world, both people and the natural world were often afflicted with plagues. The plagues were due, in large part, to highly contagious epidemics caused by unsanitary conditions, as well as other natural illnesses that spread from one person to another from a variety of untreated infections. People thought that other plagues were caused by divine intervention. Specifically, they thought that God had caused various types of sufferings to both human and nonhuman life in order to punish humankind for its infidelity and transgressions. For some of the ancient people, the plagues became a means to salvation and liberation; for others, and for the natural world, the plagues had a more devastating effect. Exodus 7:14—12:42 describes this double sense of the plagues, and invites the community of believers today to ponder deeper questions of justice with respect to the expression of divine justice and its inherent violence that the biblical text presents as a means to one people's liberation from unjust oppression by another.[6]

According to Exodus 1:8—7:13, the Israelite people, who migrated and settled in the land of Egypt, are now being oppressed by the Egyptian ruler, the Pharaoh, and those under his command. The Israelites groan to God, who hears and responds to them by raising up Moses, who will lead the Israelites out of oppression, through the wilderness, and toward the promised land. The exodus from Egypt begins with God hardening Pharaoh's heart so that a series of events could take place—the plagues—uninterruptedly. The plagues were supposed to chastise the Egyptians, show forth the absolute power and sovereignty of Israel's God, and demonstrate to the Israelites themselves that indeed their God is a God of justice and liberation who not only takes note of their suffering but who also acts to alleviate it.

Exodus 7:14–25 describes the first plague: the pollution of the Nile River and all of the other Egyptian water supplies.[7] This is the first act of punishment that, according to the text, God orchestrates against Pharaoh and his people on behalf of the Israelites. Verses 21 and 24 outline the effects of the Nile's pollution:

> And the fish in the river died. The river stank so that the Egyptians could not drink its water, and there was blood throughout the whole land of Egypt... And all the Egyptians had to dig along the Nile for water to drink, for they could not drink the water of the river.

Pharaoh's response to the event and to his own magicians reveals the character of his person: "Pharaoh turned and went into his house, and he did not take even this to heart" (v. 23). Divine justice has been executed; Israel's oppression is being avenged by its God; and Pharaoh could care less, and is without concern even for his own people, not to mention the harm done to the fish who suffer the harshest of consequences of Israel's God's action: they die.

The story of the second plague—frogs—is recounted in Exodus 8:1–15.[8] Like the first plague, God is also responsible for this one, and acts on Israel's behalf through Moses and Aaron. Following the infestation of frogs, Pharaoh pleads with Moses to pray to God to take them away. Moses honors Pharaoh's request, and God responds to Moses' intercessory prayer. The frogs die, are gathered into heaps, leaving the land stinking, with Pharaoh returning to his hardness of heart and nonresponsive attitude.

The third plague—gnats—is described in Exodus 8:16–19. This plague covers the whole land of Egypt. They came "on humans and animals alike; all the dust of the earth turned into gnats throughout the whole land of Egypt" (v. 17).[9] Verse 18 reinforces how this plague affected both human and nonhuman life: "There were gnats on both humans and animals." Still, Pharaoh's heart remains hardened even after his own magicians tell him that this plague was "the finger of God" (v. 19).

Justice and Liberation Attained through Violence 15

Following the occurrence of the gnats is the arrival of a great swarm of flies, the fourth plague (Ex. 8:20–32). The flies affect not only Pharaoh and his officials, but also the Egyptian people, and, ultimately, "In all of Egypt the land was ruined because of the flies" (v. 24). Thus, divine justice had a lethal effect on both humans and the natural world, but not on the Israelites and the land of Goshen because, according to the story, God had made "a distinction" (v. 23). And Pharaoh's heart remains hardened.

Exodus 9:1–7 depicts the fifth plague, a pestilence that attacks the Egyptians' livestock: their horses, donkeys, camels, herds, and flocks (vv. 3, 6). The biblical text makes clear that "the hand of the Lord" had done this (v. 2), and also portrays God as, once again, making a "distinction"—this time between the livestock of Israel and the livestock of Egypt (v. 4). This "distinction" spares the Israelites' livestock from the deadly plague. Divine justice has struck; the natural world has felt its direct effects, and, indirectly, so have the Egyptians. And Pharaoh's heart remains hardened.

The sixth plague, boils, takes place in Exodus 9:8–12. Once again, Moses follows God's commands. He throws down dust over the land of Egypt, which causes "festering boils on humans and animals throughout the whole land of Egypt" (v. 9). As in the case of the other plagues, only the Egyptians and their animals are affected, and this time Egypt's magicians are included in the fiasco (v. 11). Divine justice has left its mark; and Pharaoh's heart remains hardened.

Exodus 9:13–35 describes thunder and hail, the seventh plague. This passage, more than any of the other plague accounts, highlights in a personal way the character of God, who, according to the biblical text: (1) wants the Israelite people set free so that they can "worship me" (v. 13); (2) is responsible for sending the plagues to assert "my" sovereignty "in all the earth" (v. 14); (3) is interested in making known "my power," and making "my name resound through all the earth" (v. 16); (4) is feared by some Egyptians and ignored by others (vv. 20–21); (5) shows partiality to the Israelites, particularly in the land of Goshen (v. 26); and (6) responds positively to God's people's pleas, namely, Moses' request on behalf of a conniving Pharaoh, that the thunder and hail cease (vv. 33–34). Like the other plagues, this one affects humans—the Egyptians—and the natural world: the animals and the plants of the field (v. 25), including the flax and the barley (v. 31). God's justice, once again, has terrifying effects, and still, Pharaoh's heart remains hardened (v. 35).

The eighth plague, locusts, occurs in Exodus 10:1–20. Verse 15 provides a graphic picture of the devastation that this plague incurred:

> They covered the surface of the whole land, so that the land was black; and they ate all the plants in the land and all the fruit of the trees that the hail had left; nothing green was left, no tree, no plant in the field, in all the land of Egypt.

Thus, another plague sent by God as a form of divine justice causes harm to both people and the natural world. At this point, one would think that Pharaoh's heart would soften enough to let the Israelites go free, but this does not happen since God continues to harden Pharaoh's heart (v. 20). From the biblical text, readers can see that God, as portrayed by the biblical writers, is responsible for the social and environmental disasters.

The ninth plague is darkness (Ex. 10:21–29). This plague covers the earth for three days, causing the Egyptian people discomfort (v. 23), but none was suffered by the Israelites, who had light where they lived (v. 23). Through it all, Pharaoh's heart remained hardened because God had made it so (v. 27).

The final and most treacherous of all the plagues occurs in Exodus 11:1–10; 12:29–32. Verses 11:1–10 depict Moses delivering the message of God's impending judgment, and 12:29–32 describe the fulfillment of that judgment. This time, God's justice is most severe:

Justice and Liberation Attained through Violence 17

> Every firstborn in the land of Egypt shall die, from the firstborn of Pharaoh who sits on his throne to the firstborn of the female slave who is behind the handmill, and all the firstborn of the livestock. Then there will be a loud cry throughout the whole land of Egypt, such as has never been or will ever be again. But not a dog shall growl at any of the Israelites—not at people, not at animals—so that you may know the LORD makes a distinction between Egypt and Israel. (11:5–7)

> At midnight the LORD struck down all the firstborn in the land of Egypt, from the firstborn in the land of Egypt, from the firstborn of Pharaoh who sat on his throne to the firstborn of the prisoner who was in the dungeon, and all the firstborn of the livestock. (12:29)

After this tragedy had occurred, Pharaoh finally set the Israelites free; the text no longer mentions his hardness of heart.

The plague narratives make clear three essential points: first, Israel's God is a God of justice who will not tolerate injustice; second, Israel's God is a God who hears the cries of the oppressed and acts directly and indirectly to remedy the oppressive situation; and third, the stories as a whole are told from a Jewish perspective that celebrates the Jewish people's faith in a God whom they have come to know and understand as a God of faithful, salvific love, and, ultimately, a God of liberation.

For readers today, especially if they are part of believing communities, the portrayal of God's justice invites continued theological and hermeneutical reflection. The Exodus plague narratives portray God's justice as wrathful and punitive. According to the text, Pharaoh holds the power in Egypt, and both he and his officials are responsible for the Israelites' oppression. In order to counter this oppression, Pharaoh's heart is described as being "hardened" by God so that God's power over Pharaoh and the Egyptians could be asserted. If Pharaoh's heart had not been hardened, perhaps he would have freed the Israelites a long time before the last plague had struck. Because of Pharaoh's and his officials' inordinate use of power, many ordinary Egyptian people suffer at the hands of Israel's God while their leader remains nonresponsive to their plight because he himself is also under a divine spell. Furthermore and even worse, the natural world, a neutral character, is also made to suffer and bear the burden of the abusive use of power that caused unnecessary oppression to another group of people, the Israelites. One way of dealing with the oppressor is to cut off the oppressor's food supply and that of his people. A contemporary equivalent to this deed is the use of sanctions. A disconcerting point, made by the biblical text, however, is that God is said to have struck the land, animals, and plants of the Egyptians.

In summary, the plague narratives are told from a certain religious perspective and reflect the fantastic and conditioned historical and religious imagination of their writers. The God of punitive justice needs to be understood in light of the ancient concept of justice and its various cultural and social ideologies and persuasions, as well as the peoples' religious beliefs and mores that influenced their perceptions of God's justice and that continue to influence people's perceptions of God's justice today. And what remains a controversial issue for many contemporary believers today is the use of violence to stop oppression that has gotten completely out of control, which affects the innocent on both sides of the situation, inclusive of nonhuman life forms.

Finally, the biblical text as it stands seems to legitimize the use of violence to counteract injustice, especially in its portrayal of divine justice. One is left with a simple question: "Is this expression of justice truly just, especially in light of the divine eschatological vision presented in Isaiah 2:2–4 and Micah 4:1–5?" Or, is it an expression of justice reflective of the culture of its day? These and other questions call for ongoing discernment for the sake of praxis and faith that can be informed by the biblical tradition.

The Book of Judith: Justice for Holofernes

The book of Judith was written in the second century B.C.E. Its main purpose was to offer the Jewish community a sense of hope and encouragement during a time of crisis marked by fear from having to live life under the reign of Syria's Antiochus IV, who forced the Jewish people to compromise their tradition. The historical content of the book lacks accuracy with respect to the sequence of events that take place in the story and the actual dates when such events did occur. Thus, the author of the book of Judith has not written a historical account but rather has created a marvelous story based on a series of historical events, all of which are intended to reassure the Jewish people that, indeed, salvation—and not annihilation—is their lot.[10]

The book opens with the Jewish people facing terrible danger from their two strongest enemy nations, the Assyrians and the Babylonians. The story has King Nebuchadnezzar as the ruler of Assyria, and General Holofernes as the leader of the Assyrian army. Holofernes became a major threat to Judith and her people. In actuality, Nebuchadnezzar was the ruler of the Babylonians, and by the time the book of Judith was written, the Assyrians had already destroyed the Northern Kingdom of Israel in 722 B.C.E., and the Southern Kingdom of Judah with its temple and capital city of Jerusalem had already fallen to the Babylonians in 587 B.C.E.

The book's first seven chapters describe the social, religious, and political struggles the Israelites had to endure on account of Nebuchadnezzar and Holofernes. Judith as a character does not emerge until chapter 8, and from then on through chapter 16, she remains the focal point of the story. Chapters 9—16 outline her plot—and its fulfillment—to avenge the Israelites of the injustices being done to them by the Assyrians and their leaders.

Following a description of Judith's character in chapter 8, chapter 9 opens with her crying out to God with a loud voice. She first acknowledges the greatness of God's power and justice (9:2–6), and then lays out quite candidly before God the situation of the Assyrians and how she wants God to act, through her, on behalf of the Israelites (9:7–10). The chapter closes with her affirming further God's power, while calling on God to hear her prayer and empower her words so that through their deceitfulness, she will be able to accomplish what needs to be done for her people. Her final statement appeals to God's sovereignty and shows her cleverness at cajoling God to act in her favor: "Let your whole nation and every tribe know and understand that you are God, the God of all power and might, and that there is no other who protects the people of Israel but you alone!" (v. 14).

This hierarchical understanding of God as sovereign and all-powerful reflects the cultural and religious attitudes of the day, attitudes that were heavily influenced by the development of the monarchy and the growing strength of the leaders of the various nations surrounding Israel with whom the Israelites came in contact throughout the course of their history in the ancient world.

Chapter 10 features Judith preparing to carry out her deceitful plan that would gain her access to Holofernes (vv. 1–10). Events begin to reach a crescendo when she is captured by an Assyrian patrol that takes her to Holofernes (vv. 11–23). Chapters 11—12 describe the unfolding dynamics that take place between Judith and Holofernes, which eventually result in his death (chapter 13). Judith uses her beauty and charm to seduce Holofernes to the point where she is invited to his banquet. This leads to her enticing him and arousing his passion as she lies on lambskins before him after everyone has left the banquet (12:13–16). Together, they imbibe more wine, with him drinking more than he had ever drunk in his entire life (12:17–20), to the point where he becomes "dead drunk" (13:2).

Chapter 13 is the climax of the book. With Holofernes "dead drunk" and stretched out in his bed with no one in the tent with him except Judith, she now has the opportunity to take justice into her own hands. After saying a brief prayer to God in which she asks for God to "look in this hour on the work of [her] hands for the exaltation of Jerusalem"(v. 4), and to help her carry out her plan "to destroy the enemies" who have risen up against her people (v. 5), Judith proceeds to take down Holofernes' sword hanging above his bedpost and to chop off his head (vv. 6–8). After taking care of his dead body, she gives his head to her maid, who puts it in her food bag (vv. 8–10). The remainder of the chapter recounts how she shares the news with her people in the besieged city of Bethulia. There she praises God, shows the people Holofernes' head, listens to her people praise God, and then receives the praise of Uzziah, one of her elders, for her prowess.

Chapters 14–15 describe the outcome of the discovery of Holofernes' death, the flight of the now frightened Assyrians, and the exuberance of the celebratory Israelites who have now, through Judith, been liberated from Assyrian control. In chapter 16, Judith and all her people sing a hymn of praise to God, acknowledging God's divine role of justice in the whole situation that has transpired. The hymn recounts the story's events and ends with a prophetic warning:

> Woe to the nations that rise up against my people!
> The LORD the Almighty will take vengeance on them in
>   the day of judgment;
> he will send fire and worms into their flesh;
>   they shall weep in pain forever. (v. 17).

The chapter closes with a narrator's comment on Judith's renown, her graceful growth into old age, and her eventual death (vv. 21–25).

Looking at the character Judith in the context of the entire narrative, Alice Ogden Bellis observes:

> Judith is a new woman... Not only is she independent. Not only is she able to act in ways that are thought of as feminine and masculine. She is also able to give of herself in ways that are public, constructive, and self-chosen. She gives of herself, not because it is her role to be the supportive wife and mother or because she has little choice. She gives of herself, not simply in the domestic sphere. She gives of herself, using her mind, her feminine charms, and her masculine military prowess. She gives of herself to achieve for the public good what no one else in her town dared to imagine. She risks much, both in terms of her virtue with Holofernes and her reputation back home where her actions are most unusual. She comes out the victor and with her all her compatriots win.[11]

Thus, in her time and social world as represented by the biblical writer, Judith was a "heroine." She successfully liberated her people from the fear and oppression they were experiencing from the Assyrians. Her way of dealing with the whole situation was both clever and astute. Praised for her prowess, she embodied all the characteristics that one would hope to find in a "wise woman" and a "strong man." Whether or not the way she gave of herself was "constructive," in the fullest sense of the word, is open for discussion in light of how she handled the situation with Holofernes. According to the biblical narrative, justice was served when Judith lopped off Holofernes' head. This act ended the violence being done to the Israelites, but for contemporary readers today the way in which Judith achieved liberation for her people invites further theological and hermeneutical reflection. An end to the violence of injustice has been achieved through violence, heralded as courage and prowess, with God's help besought to accomplish the deed.

The book of Judith reflects a past situation that continues to occur today in similar ways and to similar people in similar

Justice and Liberation Attained through Violence 23

social locations. The web of injustice, and the use of violence needed to curb or end it, continues into the present moment. However, history shows that it has neither been curbed nor ended; rather, it has increased in a myriad of insidious ways. Therefore, readers of the Judith text, inclusive of the community of believers, must face a hard question: Is Judith's way of justice truly the way to lasting peace and liberation for all concerned?[12]

Isaiah 13—23: Justice for the Nations

Perhaps one of the most powerful descriptions of divine justice is found in Isaiah 13—23, a series of prophetic proclamations delivered by the poet Isaiah. For the most part, the proclamations are directed against countries other than Israel, though Israel, and specifically Judah, does not escape mention.[13] In several of the proclamations, readers encounter the power of God, the warrior, who metes out justice to the various countries. The divine action serves as a sign that Israel's God is also God of the nations, who will not tolerate arrogance or injustice. The poet's message of doom encompasses ten different countries or cities other than Israel: (1) Babylon (13:1–22; 14:3–23; 21:1–10); (2) Assyria (14:24–27); (3) Philistia (14:28–32); (4) Moab (15:1—16:14); (5) Damascus (17:1–3); (6) Ethiopia (18:1–7); (7) Egypt (19:1–17); (8) Dumah (21:11–12); (9) Arabia (21:13–17); and (10) Tyre (23:1–18).

Isaiah 13:1–22; 14:3–23; 21:1–10: Proclamation Concerning Babylon

In the sixth century B.C.E., Babylon was a superpower that destroyed Jerusalem and the temple, causing the downfall of the Southern Kingdom of Judah in 587 B.C.E., a situation that resulted in the exile. Isaiah 13:1–22 features the poet Isaiah delivering a chilling message to the Babylonians. Following a superscription (v. 1), the passage opens with God telling Isaiah to give a signal to the mighty army that God has summoned to come forth to execute God's judgment against the Babylonians on account of their arrogance and insolence (vv. 2–3, 11). The Medes are the ones who will execute divine judgment (v. 17), and God will serve as the commander-in-chief (v. 4c). The day of battle will be "the day of the Lord" deigned by God (v. 6), a day "cruel, with wrath and fierce anger" aimed at making the earth a "desolation" and destroying "its sinners from it" (v. 9).

The Medes whom God will stir up against the Babylonians are a proud people themselves (v. 3) and, more significantly, they are a ruthless group of warriors. In verses 14–18, the poet, speaking on behalf of God, describes first the Medes' effect on the Babylonians and then the Medes' cold-bloodedness:

> Like a hunted gazelle,
>   or like a sheep with no one to gather them,
> all will turn to their own people,
>   and all will flee to their own lands.
> Whoever is found will be thrust through,
>   and whoever is caught will fall by the sword.
> Their infants will be dashed to pieces
>   before their eyes;
> their houses will be plundered,
>   and their wives ravished.
> See, I am stirring up the Medes against them,
>   who have no regard for silver
>   and do not delight in gold.
> Their bows will slaughter the young men;
>   they will have no mercy on the fruit of the womb;
>   their eyes will not pity children.

Following this, in verses 19–22, the poet foreshadows how Babylon will become a desolation, inhabitable only to wild animals.

The proclamation against Babylon continues in Isaiah 14:3–23, where readers learn of the impending downfall of the king of Babylon, who remains unnamed.[14] This passage is a taunt song that uses past tense to relate an episode yet to happen. The use of past tense in this way is a device in Hebrew known as the prophetic perfect; it assures listeners, readers, and rereaders of the text that what the poet is foreshadowing will indeed happen. Babylon's king comes under divine judgment because he has destroyed his land and killed his people (v. 20), in addition to being extremely proud (vv. 13–14). God's wrath will befall not only the king but also his sons because of their father's guilt.[15] Thus, his bloodline, or descendants, will be wiped out (vv. 21–23).

Isaiah 21:1–10 seals the fateful doom of Babylon. Here the poet delivers a vivid vision: "Fallen, fallen is Babylon" (v. 9b), a vision that does become an historical reality when Babylon falls to Cyrus in 539 B.C.E.

The picture of God described to readers in these three passages seems to reflect a basic theological assertion that runs through all of the texts of the Prophets—namely, that God is the Lord of creation, and the Lord of history, and the Lord of hosts who is head over all. In the ancient world, when Israel and other countries were ruled by powerful monarchs and leaders who often exercised their power by means of military force, this image of warrior God as King of kings and Lord of lords would seem, perhaps, not uncommon to some of the people of ancient times. Because of this view of God, all inevitable historical events—whether good or bad—were attributed to God as described by the biblical writers and attested to in the biblical text. That Babylon receives its "just deserts" is clear from the three Isaiah passages. But the description of this execution of divine justice portrayed by these texts needs further comment. First, according to Isaiah 13:1–22, God uses a people, the Medes, who are just as proud and powerful—if not more so—as the Babylonians to mete out to them a divine justice that is full of wrath. Tones of *lex talionis* seem to undergird this expression of justice. Second, this passage depicts God using the brute force of another nation (Isaiah 13:17–19) to chastise Babylon (Isaiah 13:6–12). And third, in the midst of such chastisement, vulnerable and innocent lives are affected and lost: infants (Isa. 13:16a); women (Isa. 13:16b); and children (Isa. 13:18,

14:20b–21). A bold question faces contemporary readers: "What kind of God is Israel's God who would use the vicious power of one nation to chastise—and eventually destroy—another for the sake of justice?" Or is this picture of God and God's justice portrayed in the Isaiah texts influenced by the theological, cultural, social, and political situation of the prophet's day? Finally, these three biblical texts in their canonical form seem to reflect a picture of violence embedded within them.

Isaiah 14:24–27: Proclamation Concerning Assyria

In the eighth century B.C.E., Assyria was the great superpower pitted against the Northern Kingdom. In 722 B.C.E., Assyria successfully destroyed Israel and deported its people. Verse 25 is the climax of the passage. Here God through the poet reveals the divine plan against Assyria:

> I will break the Assyrian in my land,
> and on my mountains trample him underfoot;
> his yoke shall be removed from them,
> and his burden from their shoulders.

No longer will Israel, or any other nation, have to suffer the yoke and burden of imperial oppression caused by Assyria. God's assertion of power over one nation will be a source of liberation and security for another. The Isaiah passage, however, reflects divine power being used aggressively and characterized by language of destruction: "I will break the Assyrian..." The text invites contemporary readers to reflect on how liberation will be achieved, and whether or not this way of securing justice for other nations is the way of divine justice.

Isaiah 14:28–32: Proclamation Concerning Philistia

The superscription of this proclamation (v. 1) places it in the time of the eighth century B.C.E. The Philistia nation consisted of five city-states, each with their own king. As a people, the Philistines were Judah's neighbors who were always looking for ways to get Judah to trust in them for deliverance from its enemies instead of trusting in God to do this. The occasion for this proclamation is Philistia's rejoicing over the apparent death of one of its oppressors who seems to have been one of the Assyrian rulers.[16] This death would mean the Philistines' liberation from Assyrian rule, but Isaiah reminds the people that the worst is yet to come:

> The firstborn of the poor will graze,
>   and the needy lie down in safety;
> but I will make your root die of famine,
>   and your remnant I will kill.
>   (v. 30)

God will deal with Philistia. The verse foreshadows some sort of military invasion that will leave Philistia devastated (v. 31) and, thus, Judah safe. Such an ill-fated fortune that is to befall Philistia is credited to the work of God. Hence, Judah's future security will be obtained through violence that, according to the biblical text, is sanctioned by God.

Isaiah 15:1—16:14: Proclamation Concerning Moab

This proclamation seems to reflect an eighth-century B.C.E. setting similar to that of the two previous Isaiah passages. Moab was a region on the East side of the Dead Sea, and extended to the Arnon River. In general, the country posed no great threat to Israel. However, as John N. Oswalt notes:

> [That] both nations laid claim to the lands north of the Arnon (the land of Ammon which was given to Reuben and Gad, Num. 32:1–5; 33–38) was a continuing source of conflict between them (Num. 21:24–30; Judg. 3:12–30; 11:22–26; 1 Sam. 14:47; 2 Kings 3:4–27) until there was ultimately a deep hostility (Zeph. 2:9, 10).[17]

Chapter 15:1–9 is a lament. Here the poet describes for listeners and readers the unexpected disaster that is about to befall Moab, turning a nation into a group of refugees. The event happens at night, and Moab's enemies go unnamed. Chapter

16:1–5 appears to be a plea: the Moabites seek help from Judah; specifically, they desire refuge in the Southern Kingdom, and "look forward to a day when oppression ceases and the Davidic throne is secure, issuing such justice and righteousness on behalf of all."[18] But Judah's response in verses 6–12 is harsh:

> We have heard of the pride of Moab
> —how proud he is!—
> of his arrogance, his price, and his insolence;
> his boasts are false.
> Therefore let Moab wail,
> let everyone wail for Moab.
> Mourn, utterly stricken'
> for the raisin cakes of Kir-haraseth.
> (vv. 6–7)

Verses 8–12 continue Judah's response; the poet laments the sad state of Moab after its invasion. Such a description gives rise to "the suspicion...that the lamentation masks a taunt for what is considered a well-deserved come-down."[19]

Verses 12–13 predict the fulfillment of the proclamation declared against Moab in 15:1—16:11. In verse 12 the poet makes clear that when Moab resorts to his god for relief, his efforts will have been done in vain. In verse 13, the poet delivers a divine verdict to Moab that foreshadows the complete demise of the country. Thus, "Moab will cease to be a formidable presence and will therefore become a helpless pawn in the drama of power politics."[20]

Isaiah 15:1—16:14 describes a tough blow that Moab will have to endure: devastation by unnamed enemies; no help from a could-be ally; no response from its god; and a verdict of doom from Israel's God. All this is due to Moab's arrogance, pride, insolence, and boasting. The cliché, "Pride goeth before the fall," seems befitting for Moab, and readers of the biblical text are faced with another example of justice that leaves a country reduced to desperation: "those who survive will be very few and feeble" (Isa. 16:14).

Isaiah 17:1–3: Proclamation Concerning Damascus

Damascus, the capital of Syria, is the focus of Isaiah 17:1–3. The fact that it was taken and ravaged by Tiglath-Pileser III in 732 B.C.E. suggests an eighth-century B.C.E. setting for this text. In these verses, the poet announces the forthcoming destruction of Damascus. Isaiah 7:8 and Amos 1:3–5 hint at the reason for Damascus' impending demise: Damascus, fearful of the looming power of Assyria, sought security by means of an "armed alliance with Aram (see 7:7–9)."[21] Additionally, Damascus was guilty of crimes of terror done against other people (see Am. 1:3–5). Thus, Damascus will suffer ruin by the hands of another country, with God suggesting through the poet Isaiah that indeed Damascus' ruination is the price the city will pay for not placing its trust in Israel's God, and for having committed heinous crimes.[22] According to Isaiah 17:1–3, justice will be served, but the type of justice that the text foreshadows is punitive, violent, and destructive. Contemporary readers are left to ponder the effectiveness of this type of justice.

Isaiah 18:1–7: Proclamation Concerning Ethiopia

Of all the proclamations made to the various nations thus far, Isaiah 18:1–7 is perhaps the most obscure. Verses 1–2 and 7 pertain specifically to Ethiopia; verses 3–5 address the world's inhabitants. The proclamation focuses on the power and sovereignty of God. The first two verses suggest that Ethiopia is involved in diplomatic relations with other countries, with verse 2 describing the Ethiopians in particular: "a nation tall and smooth," "a people feared near and far," and "a nation mighty and conquering." Ethiopia is regarded as a nation with military prowess and strength. In light of verses 3–6, this description becomes ironic.

Addressed to people globally, verses 3–6 describe a warrior God who eyes Ethiopia from afar and who, like a harvester, will nip Ethiopia's strength in the bud, leaving the Ethiopians as food for the birds of prey and the animals of the earth. Such is the sight all the inhabitants of the world will see; such is the lesson they will learn: that power and sovereignty belong to God and God alone, to whom the remnant of Ethiopia will bring gifts (v. 7). This passage depicts God using divine power to establish divine sovereignty over "a nation mighty and conquering." Not long would this nation be one feared among others. Justice will be established among nations, and a worldwide lesson will be taught, but at what cost to the Ethiopians?

Isaiah 19:1–17: Proclamation Concerning Egypt

With a vivid imagination, the poet describes the wicked plan that God has concocted against Egypt, one of the superpowers of the ancient world, viewed by other countries as a destabilizing force that, in time, would need to be reckoned with. Isaiah's vision pictures God riding on a swift cloud—the storm god image—coming to cast judgment on Egypt. The effects of God's presence in Egypt will be terrifying: (1) Egypt's idols will tremble at the divine presence (v. 1); (2) The Egyptians' hearts will melt within them (v. 1); (3) the people will turn against each other (v. 2); (4) they will become dispirited (v. 3); and (5) they will be delivered into "the hand of a hard master; / a fierce king will rule over them" (v. 4). Brueggemann notes, "What goes around comes around! Now it is Egypt's turn to be subservient and exploited."[23] If this passage is dated to the eighth century B.C.E., then the "hard master" and "fierce king" could be any of the Assyrians' anticipated overlords, beginning with Tiglath-Pilesar III to Ashurbanipal.

Not only will the Egyptians be affected by the divine plan, but also will the natural world:

> The waters of the Nile will be dried up,
>   and the river will be parched dry;
> its canals will become foul,
>   and the branches of Egypt's Nile will diminish and dry up,
>   reeds and rushes will rot away.
> There will be bare places by the Nile,
>   on the brink of the Nile;

and all that is sown by the Nile will dry up,
    be driven away, and be no more.
    (vv. 5–7)

Even the fish and the blossom of the field will be destroyed, causing a setback in the nation's economy. None of Egypt's trusted leaders, counselors, and sages will be able to remedy the situation (vv. 11–15). The one with power and strength over Egypt will be Judah.

This passage brings good news to God's own people, the Judahites, but to the Egyptians it is a message of doom. Once again readers see God being depicted as all-powerful and sovereign, and using the divine power to secure one country at grave cost to another. In the process of such assertion of power, other non-involved aspects of life are made to suffer so as to create a ripple effect that would, in turn, add to the devastation of the Egyptian people. Divine power puts in check human power, but through what means, and for what purpose: the assertion of sovereignty? (v. 4); the establishment of particularity? (v. 17). Furthermore, the gender-specific metaphor in verse 16 suggests a bias and admits a distasteful slur: "On that day the Egyptians will be like women, and tremble with fear before the hand that the LORD of hosts raises against them."

Isaiah 19:1–17 invites contemporary readers to evaluate how God and God's actions are portrayed by the text, as well as how women are viewed with respect to the text's metaphorical language. The inherent violence embedded within the text's theological message and literary composition set the tone for raising questions from an ethical perspective with regard to the "justness" of God's plan and its execution as depicted by the text.

Isaiah 21:11–12: Proclamation Concerning Dumah

Different from the other proclamations included in Isaiah 13—23, Isaiah 21:11–12 does not include any mention of divine intentions. To the contrary, this text has a historical import:

Given the historical background in relation to Sennacherib's conquest of Dumah or Dumat al-Jandal in 689, a major oasis and Arab religious center on the caravan routes through the north Arabian desert, it becomes clear that the watchman's report is intended to indicate the fall of Dumah to Sennacherib's forces.[24]

Viewing the passage's context as a poem sandwiched between 21:1–10 and 21:13–17, both of which attribute the fall of Babylon and the defeat of Kedar to God, one could postulate that the fall of Dumah was the result of God's actions as well.[25] Thus, the exercise of divine power becomes the means for creating weal and woe that results in the devastation of a people, its land, and the country as a whole. This passage calls readers to consider how the power of God is being portrayed by the biblical text, and whether or not this portrait reflects a sense of justice, in light of the effects of the use of such power.

Isaiah 21:13–17: Proclamation Concerning Kedar

This passage consists of two units, verses 13b–15 and verses 16–17. In the first unit, the poet addresses two groups of people—the Dedonites (v. 13) and the Temanites (v. 14)—who have assisted fugitives in Arabia. In the second unit, the poet reveals what has been spoken to him by God specifically: that Kedar will come to an end because God has deemed it so (v. 17). Here, as in the other earlier proclamations, the demise of a country is attributed to the power and intention of God. Furthermore, the canonical text of Isaiah 21:13–17 seems to affirm the use of power in this way and thus sparks an ethical question for contemporary readers to ponder: "How just is power when it is used destructively as this Isaiah text suggests?"

Isaiah 23:1–18: Proclamation Concerning Tyre

The last in a series of proclamations envisioning the downfall of great and small countries alike, this proclamation announces the fate of Tyre. The first part of the poem describes Tyre's fall

(vv. 1–14); the second part foreshadows its restoration and allegiance to God (vv. 15–18). God will chastise Tyre because of its pride (v. 9). Verse 11 makes clear that God is the force behind Tyre's destruction (v. 11a) and that God orders the destruction (v. 11b). The picture comes into sharper focus in verse 13: Babylon is the human agent through whom God will accomplish the predetermined task. Verse 14 calls for lamentation; indeed, Tyre will be destroyed. Again, the poet delivers the proclamation in the prophetic perfect tense, which is a device used to assure his listeners that what has been proclaimed will happen.

The passage closes on a note of optimism. Although Tyre will be "forgotten for seventy years" (v. 15), after that time "the Lord will visit Tyre" (v. 17), which, in turn, will experience a new spirit of dedication to God and generosity toward all those "who live in the presence of the Lord" (v. 18).

Isaiah 23:1–18 is remarkable insofar as it speaks of divine chastisement and the transformation that results from it. Readers see from the text that severe, punitive chastisement has the potential for bringing about a change of heart. The text as it stands seems to sanction the use of violence as a means for rectifying and changing difficult situations, and to suggest to readers an image of God as a God of terror, who is to be feared. This view of divine chastisement and its portrait of God provides a backdrop for ongoing critical theological reflection in a contemporary world that struggles to learn new and nonviolent ways to deal with the daily challenges of inordinate pride, arrogance, oppression, and injustice.

In summary, the ten proclamations concerning the various nations reflect the cultural and social attitudes of their day and those of their authors and later editors. The underlying theological assertions that each of the passages make—as well as the picture of God that they collectively portray—also reflect the cultural and social worlds of the authors and editors. The divine plan that calls for nations not to assert unjust power over each other needs to be affirmed, but how the divine plan is put into practice needs further ethical consideration. God's justice in Isaiah 13—23 seems to resemble the kind of justice articulated by *lex talionis* and the belief in the deuteronomistic theology of retribution. This expression of justice falls short of embracing the vision articulated in Isaiah 2:2-4 that features God acting as an arbitrator, which leads to swords being turned into plowshares and spears into pruning hooks, with nation not lifting sword against nation, and neither learning war anymore. Reading Isaiah 13—23 against the grain of Isaiah 2:2-4 provides readers with fertile soil for fruitful conversation on the topics of God, power, and justice.

Jeremiah 5

The theme of justice and retribution continues in Jeremiah 5. In this passage, justice takes the form of punitive chastisement. This text is an indictment against Jerusalem and Judah: the people are guilty of apostasy and idolatry (vv. 6-7) coupled by smug religious pride and arrogance (v. 12). Even the prophets and priests have corrupted their offices and have forsaken their religious responsibilities to the people (vv. 13, 30-31). Verses 1-6, the first unit, form a standard lawsuit that describes the depravity of these Judahites from among both the poor and the rich. Divine judgment comes in verse 6:

> Therefore a lion from the forest shall kill them,
>   a wolf from the desert shall destroy them.
> A leopard is watching against their cities;
>   everyone who goes out of them shall be torn in pieces—
> because their transgressions are many,
>   their apostasies are great.

This gruesome vision of judgment, also seen as the implementation of divine justice, foreshadows verses 14-17, a second expression of divine justice. Verses 14-17 describe God metaphorically as a warrior God—"The God of hosts" (v. 14)—who, as Commander-in-Chief of the nations, pledges to bring another nation against Judah. This invading nation will destroy Judah (vv. 15-17).

This divine judgment against Judah, which brings with it the promise of punitive chastisement, in turn becomes an expression of divine justice magnified by three simple questions:

[1] How can I pardon you? (v. 7)
[2] Shall I not punish them for these things?...
[3] and shall I not bring retribution on a nation such as this? (v. 9)

God is infuriated with the people, and they will be made to pay for their offenses and transgressions. This is a classic example of divine retribution that has often been interpreted as God's justice.

Verses 18–19, the third unit, offer a brief word of hope (v. 18), followed by a striking example of *lex talionis*: "And when your people say, 'Why has the LORD our God done all these things to us?' you shall say to them, 'As you have forsaken me and served foreign gods in your land, so you shall serve strangers in a land that is not yours'" (v. 19). The message is clear: God is about to turn the tables on the Judahites.

The last part of the passage contains a series of images (vv. 20–31). God commands the prophet to deliver a lengthy message to the people, which the prophet does. In this message, God enumerates all of Judah's faults, the worst of which is the lack of justice toward the orphan and the failure to defend the rights of the needy (v. 28). The double question posed earlier is now repeated: "Shall I not punish them for these things?... / and shall I not bring retribution / on a nation such as this?" (v. 29). Divine wrath remains kindled against Judah.

Historically, military invasion against Judah, and the eventual demise of both Jerusalem and the Southern Kingdom, were inevitable. However, people in the ancient world understood suffering of this nature as an exercise of divine justice.

In summary, Jeremiah 5 presents a view of justice that is not only retributive and punitive but also inherently violent. It is a justice that reflects the culture and religious beliefs of its day and one that continues to find expression today in the face of increased violence and inexplicable suffering.

The vision of God as a vengeful God who metes out retribution and punitive justice is not consistent, however, among the writings of the prophets. The book of Hosea suggests an alternative view to Jeremiah's view of God and God's ways:

> How can I give you up, Ephraim?
> > How can I hand you over, O Israel?
> How can I make you like Admah?
> > How can I treat you like Zeboiim?
> My heart recoils within me;
> > my compassion grows warm and tender.
> I will not execute my fierce anger;
> > I will not again destroy Ephraim;
> for I am God and no mortal,
> > the Holy One in your midst,
> > and I will not come in wrath.
> > (Hos. 11:8–9)

Reading Jeremiah 5 against the grain of Hosea 11:8–9 and Genesis 4:1–17 confronts today's readers and believers with a challenge to find ways of expressing justice appropriately, ways that respect the inherent dignity of all life, even in the midst of egregious injustices. The prophetic call is one of justice with compassion, for divine justice is never without divine compassion (see, e.g., Mic. 7:18—20).

A New Testament Vision of Justice: Assertive and Reconciling

The vision of justice expressed by the Old Testament texts Genesis 4:1–17 and Hosea 11:8–9 finds an echo in the writings of the New Testament, where justice is more often assertive and reconciling than retributive and punitive. The New Testament writers' vision of divine justice as depicted through Jesus' words and deeds is basically nonviolent. It opposes the vision of divine justice put forth by the writers of the Old Testament and their perception of God, though this vision is not altogether consistent throughout the Old Testament, as has already been noted. Luke 18:1–8, Matthew 23:1–36, and Luke 23:26–42 offer readers a different view of justice than what is commonly seen in the Old Testament.

Luke 18:1–8: "Grant me justice against my opponent."

This marvelous and artistically crafted Lukan narrative stars three characters: Jesus, a surly judge, and a relentless widow. The narrative opens with Jesus telling his disciples a parable meant to encourage them to remain faithful to and persistent in prayer (v. 1). The judge and widow become models for the lesson Jesus is trying to teach his disciples. Jesus begins his parable in verse 2. The first character he introduces to the disciples is a judge "who neither feared God nor had respect for people" (v. 2). A stock character in this narrative, the judge was probably one of the local magistrates in both Jesus' and Luke's times. This judge resides in a city unnamed.

Also residing in the city is a widow who keeps coming to the judge saying, "Grant me justice against my opponent" (v. 3). In the social context of the first century c.e., widows were considered to be among the most vulnerable members of the society. They were also considered to be outstanding examples of devotion.[26]

The narrative's action commences with the widow's demand made to the judge. Her opponent's identity remains obscure, and thus one can only speculate that she was a plaintiff in a lawsuit in which she was denied equity. In response to the widow's demand for justice, the judge does nothing at first. Later, however, he becomes self-reflective. He acknowledges that he has no fear of God and no respect for anyone (v. 4), and also comes to the realization that if he does not act on this widow's behalf, she will wear him out "by continually coming" with her demands (v. 5). Thus, because of the nuisance the widow made of herself and her persistence, the judge decides to grant her justice (v. 5).

The judge's decision concludes Jesus' parable, and Luke continues the narrative by having Jesus teach the disciples the lesson embedded in his parable—namely, that their God is a benevolent and just God who will act quickly on their behalf when they cry out to God for justice (vv. 6–8a). Jesus' final comment, a rhetorical question, adds a twist to his teaching, and offers the disciples a challenge: "And yet, when the Son of Man comes, will he find faith on earth?" The parable of the judge and the widow becomes a story for the disciples to ponder, and a lesson for them to live out.

In summary, Luke's narrative offers a multilayered vision of justice. First, the widow acts justly on her own behalf. She knows that she has not received justice, and so she actively pursues justice for herself by seeking out a judge and demanding it. Second, the judge, who has no regard for God or human beings, does act with justice on her behalf; he grants her request and in so doing fulfills the obligation of Torah.[27] He does it simply because the widow will give him no peace otherwise. Hence, her persistence is the occasion for the judge to act justly. Third, the judge becomes a model for what God is and what God is not. Unlike the judge, God is a just God who cares about all or creation and will act with justice for all who cry out. And, unlike the judge, God acts on behalf of the most vulnerable, not because of persistence alone, but because God is forever faithful to covenant and the plight of the oppressed (see Ex. 2:23–25).

Finally, although this narrative is a lesson about prayer, it is also a lesson about justice. The widow received justice from the judge, and, in turn, the judge will be the recipient of God's fair and benevolent justice because he has helped "to loose the bonds of injustice" and "to undo the thongs of the yoke" (Isa. 58:6). Thus, Luke's narrative presents a vision of justice that is human and divine, transformative and "just" in a way that is reconciling and not punitive, hopeful and not vindictive.

Matthew 23:1–36: Words of Woe

Another story that presents a vision of justice that is both confrontational and assertive, but not violent and aggressive, is Matthew's narrative about Jesus denouncing the scribes and

Pharisees. Matthew begins his story with Jesus addressing the crowds and his disciples and teaching them two lessons: (1) that the scribes and Pharisees sit on Moses' seat, and therefore the disciples are to listen to their teachings about the law, follow their teachings, and keep the law; and (2) that they (the crowds and disciples) are not to follow the *ways* of the scribes and Pharisees because they are hypocrites—they do not practice what they teach (vv. 1–3). Jesus then goes on to explain himself by citing the various deeds of the scribes and Pharisees that go against the grain of their teachings (vv. 4–7), and then proceeds to tell his listeners how they are to act (vv. 8–10). Jesus then summarizes his entire instruction (vv. 11–12).

How Matthew depicts Jesus dealing with the scribes' and Pharisees' hypocrisy is a lesson in divine justice. With gusto, Jesus condemns the scribes and Pharisees not only for their ways that are hypocritical to their teachings (vv. 13–36) but also for their neglect of "the weightier matters of the law: justice and mercy and faith" (v. 23). Jesus points out to them that it is these that they "ought to have practiced without neglecting the others" (v. 23). Verse 23 is the heart of Jesus' condemnation. The verse is central to Matthew's message because the statement points out that the scribes and Pharisees are not only hypocritical but also unjust. Jesus' way of dealing with the dilemma of the scribes and Pharisees is not to punish them but rather to uncover verbally their deeds and to admonish them verbally: "Woe to you." By bringing their corrupt ways to light, he nonviolently but forcefully decentralizes their hierarchical power and status over the people without negating their office as teachers of the law. He also gives those who have not experienced justice and mercy from the scribes and Pharisees a sense of hope by giving voice, inferentially, to their plight.

Through Jesus' verbal condemnation of the scribes' and Pharisees' deeds and ways, the listeners of Jesus' day and today see an example of justice that is assertive and direct. They are given a model that does not condone hypocrisy or unfairness but rather confronts it in a way that focuses on the deeds themselves while preserving the integrity of all the persons concerned. Finally, the way that Jesus deals with the situation of the scribes and Pharisees sheds light on how divine justice is implemented, which, in turn, becomes a challenge for people today to act accordingly.

Luke 23:26–43: "...forgive them..."

The most poignant vision of justice that occurs in the face of the most devastating experience of injustice is recounted in Luke's gospel account of Jesus' crucifixion. This tragic event comes as no surprise: Simeon foreshadowed opposition to Jesus (Lk. 2:34–35) and Jesus himself foresaw his own death, which came as the expected consequences of his fidelity to his prophetic mission (see Lk. 4:24; 9:21–27, 43–45; 11:49–52; 18:31—34).

The climax of Luke's crucifixion narrative is not the actual event but, rather, the words that Luke has Jesus utter from the cross: "Father, forgive them; for they do not know what they are doing" (v. 34a). Betrayed by Judas (Lk. 22:47–53), denied by Peter (Lk. 22:54–62), mocked, beaten, and ordered to prophesy (Lk. 22:63–65), and finally brought to trial (Lk. 22:66—23:12) because he loved deeply and was thus compelled to deal with the injustices of his day that caused oppression to others and robbed them of the good news that God's divine plan of salvation was for all creation, this man Jesus—Son of David and Son of God—understood the essence of divine justice: compassion expressed through forgiveness. Throughout his life, as the gospel of Luke attests, Jesus never paled from confronting the injustices of his day, and he never once retreated from his mission, which was to announce that the reign of God was unfolding in the midst of all. His whole life—his preaching, his teaching, his healings, his great love for sinners and social outcasts, his tolerance of political and religious opposition to him—led him to the cross and to his final act of justice before his death: "Father, forgive them..." (Lk. 23:34).

The last episode of Luke's crucifixion narrative provides a further lesson about justice:

> One of the criminals who were hanged there kept deriding him and saying "Are you not the Messiah? Save yourself and us!" But the other rebuked him, saying, "Do you not fear God, since you are under the same sentence of condemnation? And we indeed have been condemned justly, for we are getting what we deserve for our deeds, but this man has done nothing wrong." Then he said, "Jesus, remember me when you come into your kingdom." He replied, "Truly, I tell you, today you will be with me in Paradise."(vv. 39–43)

Condemnation and the death sentence have been meted out for two criminals. They hang on crosses on both sides of Jesus. Justice has been served. The one criminal acknowledges the "justness" of both their sentences and the "unjustness" of Jesus' sentence, and then asks Jesus to remember him when Jesus comes into his kingdom. In response, Jesus promises him eternal life (v. 43).

In summary, Luke's crucifixion account presents a multifaceted picture of justice. In the case of Jesus, the scales of justice weigh against him unjustly. Though innocent of any crime, he is condemned and sentenced to die. In the case of the two criminals, the scales of justice also weigh against them, but justly so. The one criminal, however, recognizes the injustice being done to Jesus and verbalizes it. This acknowledgment is significant because it points out how flawed and biased human justice can be. Furthermore, Jesus' response to this criminal reveals the mysteriousness of divine justice, which often surpasses legal justice and defies human reason and expectations. In this story, Luke's Jesus embodies *par excellence* the face of God and the spirit of God's justice, which is the face of compassion and the spirit of forgiveness extended to all humanity, made evident through his response to the criminal's plea, and his own plea to God: "Father, forgive them: for they do not know what they are doing" (v. 34a).

Concluding Remarks

Selected passages from both the Old and New Testaments portray divine expressions of justice found within the biblical tradition. The Old Testament texts studied put forth a vision of justice that is, for the most part, retributive and punitive. In some instances, this type of justice led to the liberation of one people from the unjust oppression of another. The liberation, however, was not without cost to either human or nonhuman life, or sometimes both. Among the cultural and religious beliefs that had an influence on the Israelites' sense of justice—both human and divine—we find the *lex talionis* and the deuteronomistic theology of retribution. Thus, God was not infrequently viewed as a divine warrior, an avenging God who meted out to Israel and to the other nations their "just deserts."

Inherent in the retributive and punitive type of justice were varying degrees of violence, which ranged from brutal verbal threats by God to the chopping off of Holofernes' head by Judith. Yet, texts like Genesis 4:1–16 and Hosea 11:8–9 offer another view of justice that bespeaks of compassion. This view is found most often in the writings of the New Testament, reaching a crescendo in Luke's crucifixion account. Jesus, the one persecuted unjustly, does not treat his persecutors in kind. Rather, he intercedes to God for them, pleading for their forgiveness.

These different expressions of justice exist in the here and now, and readers of the biblical texts are challenged to retrieve from the tradition and contemporary culture a vision of justice that has as its guiding principle a respect for the intrinsic goodness that lies at the heart of all that exists. Would that people everywhere embody Isaiah's and Jesus' vision and thus embrace their prophetic vocation, which goes right to the heart of the Jewish and Christian tradition:

> Here [are] my servant[s], whom I uphold,
>   my chosen, in whom my soul delights;
> I have put my spirit upon [them];
>   [they] will bring forth justice to the nations.
> [They] will not cry or life up [their] voice,
>   or make it heard in the street;
> a bruised reed [they] will not break,
>   and a dimly burning wick [they] will not quench;
>   [they] will faithfully bring forth justice.
> [They] will not grow faint or be crushed
>   until [they have] established justice in the earth;
>   and the coastlands wait for [their] teaching.
>   (Isa. 42:1–4; cf. Mt. 12:18–21)

Such a vision and vocation pave the way for the convergence of human and divine justice that can give birth to the "new" heavens and the "new" earth promised from long ago (see Isa. 65:17–25).

CHAPTER 2

Hospitality of Heart
The Spirit of Justice

One of the central organs for the ancient Jewish people was the heart, which played a prominent role in early Christianity as well. Both the Old and New Testaments have countless references to the heart. For example, in the Torah one hears that God set God's "heart" on the Israelites and chose them despite the fact that they were the fewest of all peoples, because God loved them (Deut. 7:7–8). This same community is also asked to circumcise the foreskins of their hearts (Deut. 10:16; Jer. 4:4). In the writings of the Prophets, Jeremiah proclaims that God will put God's law within them and write it on their hearts (Jer. 31:33). Ezekiel 36:26 announces a similar divine promise: "A new heart I will give you, and a new spirit I will put within you; and I will remove from your body the heart of stone and give you a heart of flesh."

In the New Testament writings, Matthew 11:28–30 depicts Jesus extending an invitation of comfort while making reference to his own heart:

> Come to me, all you that are weary and are carrying heavy burdens, and I will give you rest. Take my yoke upon you, and learn from me; for I am gentle and humble in heart, and you will find rest for your souls. For my yoke is easy, and my burden is light.

Paul preaches that the heart is where Christ and the Spirit dwell (Eph. 3:17, 2 Cor. 1:22). The Philippians hold Paul in their hearts (Phil. 1:7); Paul proclaims to the Corinthians that his heart is wide open to them (2 Cor. 11–13).

Perhaps one of the most significant references to the heart is found in the writings of Ephraem of Syria, who, when asked by one of his brothers what compassion was, responds:

> …a heart on fire for the whole of creation, for humanity, for the birds, for the animals, for demons and for all that exists. At the recollection and at the sight of them such a person's eyes overflow with tears owing to vehemence of the compassion which grips his [or her] heart; as a result of his [or her] deep mercy his [or her] heart shrinks and cannot bear to hear or look on any injury or the slightest suffering of any thing in creation.[1]

In sum, these passages, selected from among a myriad of references to the heart found in ancient writings, call for a transformation, and speak of a sense of compassion and a sentiment of deep-felt love. The writings of Matthew and Paul in particular suggest a certain kind of "hospitality of heart."

In a global community today, where social and ecological injustice continues to cause pain and death to both human and nonhuman life, a hospitality of heart that not only welcomes all life but also works to sustain it and free it from the jaws of injustice is absolutely necessary if the web of violence is to be broken, and the vision of "new heavens / and a new earth"[2] is to be realized. This hospitality of heart can be a motivating principle for the justice that has as its starting point the recognition of the intrinsic goodness and the interrelatedness of all life as reflected in the Genesis 1—2 creation account.

Genesis 1—2: "And God saw that it was good...very good." (vv. 1:10, 12, 18, 21, 25, 31)

Traditionally viewed as two separate versions of the creation account (Gen. 1:1—2:4a, the Priestly or "P" version, and Gen. 2:4b–25, the Jahwist or "J" version), Genesis 1—2 is essentially two different stories, each with its own transmission history, that have been presented together to offer one "canonical picture of creation."[3] The vision of the intrinsic goodness of all creation, the interrelatedness of all creation, and the interdependence of all creation are central to this canonical picture of creation.

The writers of Genesis 1—2 depict God as the creator of all that exists. In Genesis 1:1—2:4a, God creates everything in six days and rests on the seventh. In the midst of recounting God's creative activities of each day, the biblical writers make it a point to say, "And God saw that it was good" (1:1—2:4a, 10, 12, 18, 21, 25). When all creation has been completed, one hears, "God saw everything that [God] had made, and indeed, it was very good" (1:31). Significant here is that creation receives the affirmation of the Divine not because it performs some task or has a specific purpose. It is "good," "very good," just because it "is"—just because it exists. Hence, the goodness of creation is not rooted in or connected to a sense of its usefulness. Creation is good just because it has been created, and for the believing community then and now, because God created it.

This understanding of the intrinsic goodness of creation relates to another major point that can be extrapolated from Genesis 1—2, specifically that all of creation is interrelated and interdependent. For example, in Genesis 2:4b–25, one hears that a human being is formed out of the dust of the "ground" (2:7); out of the "ground the Lord God made to grow every tree" (2:9); and "out of the ground the Lord God formed every animal of the field and every bird of the air" (2:19). Thus, the human being, the plants, and the animals have a common origin—the ground, which can also be understood as the earth[4]—all of which has a common divine origin: God. The creation story, then, speaks of an interrelatedness that exists between human and nonhuman life and the relationship that each has to God, and that God has with both. Furthermore, both human beings and the animals are recipients of God's blessing (1:28 and 1:22, respectively). The biblical text links the concept of blessing to the idea of procreation: "God blessed them; saying, 'Be fruitful and multiply and fill the waters in the seas, and let birds multiply on the earth'" (1:22; compare with 1:28). Hence, the biblical text suggests that both human and nonhuman life forms have the potential of participating in the divine work of creation.

Another example of interrelatedness that the creation story suggests can be found in Genesis 2:4b–5:

> In the day that the LORD God made the earth and the heavens, when no plant of the field was yet in the earth and no herb of the field had yet sprung up—for the LORD God had not caused it to rain upon the earth, and there was no one to till the ground...

The plant and herb of the field cannot sprout until the rains come upon the earth. The rain cannot water the earth until God causes the rains to happen. The earth cannot yield its vegetation until someone tills the ground, which is to be the human being's task (2:15). Thus, both human and nonhuman life, together with the Divine, have a role to play in the ongoing flourishing of creation.

Genesis 2:15 speaks of the task divinely assigned to one of the human beings: "The LORD God took the man and put him in the garden of Eden to till it and keep it." Next, one hears about God creating the animals and a second human being as helpers, as partners to the first human being (Gen. 2:18–20). These biblical verses suggest not only a sense of mutuality, but also, from a gender-specific perspective, a vision of equality between the two human beings; the male and female whom God created (cf. 1:27).[5] These verses, like others in Genesis 1—2, continue to suggest a picture of the many interrelated relationships that exist within the creation story, and that do exist within creation itself. At the heart of biodiversity is a mysterious and magnificent oneness that continues to unfold and waits to be celebrated.

In addition to having the task of tilling and caring for the garden, God gives human beings the command to have "dominion over the fish of the sea and over the birds of the air and over every living thing that moves upon the earth" (1:28), heard earlier in the text. The Hebrew word translated as "dominion" does not mean "domination," as some English interpretations of the Hebrew text have suggested. Bruce C. Birch, Walter Brueggemann, Terence E. Fretheim, and David L. Petersen make that clear:

> The command to have dominion (1:28), in which God delegates responsibility for the nonhuman creation in a power-sharing relationship with humans, must be understood in terms of care-giving, not exploitation (see the use of the verb *radah* in Ps. 72:8-14; Ezek. 34:1-4).[6]

The idea of dominion as care-giving and good governance becomes explicit in the wisdom tradition, specifically in Psalm 104:1–30, a psalm that depicts a benevolent God who cares for all creation. Within this psalm is the suggestion of an interdependence that exists among the various dimensions of creation. In the middle of the psalm is a word of praise:

> O Lord, how manifold are your works!
>   In wisdom you have made them all;
>   the earth is full of your creatures.
>   (v. 24)

Prior to this verse, the psalmist speaks about God's kindness to animals and human beings alike (see, e.g., vv. 10—23). In verse 24c, the psalmist brings together these two forms of life in a single awe-filled phrase: "the earth is full of your creatures."

In the psalmist's view, animals and human beings share a common classification: they are "creatures." As James Luther Mays notes:

It is remarkable with what unqualified directness the human species is considered as simply one of the creatures dependent on the providing of God. Homo sapiens appears in the review (vv. 14–15, 23) as simply one more kind of creature that lives on the earth in the environment it provides. Psalm 8 gives another, though not contradictory, view. But there is not a hint of anthropocentric claim here. In the praise of the creator, the human being sees itself simply as one of the creatures sustained by the providence of God.[7]

Both the animals and the human beings cohabit the earth, and the earth provides for their needs in accordance with the divine plan and work of God:

> You cause the grass to grow for the cattle,
>   and plants for people to use,
> to bring forth food from the earth,
>   and wine to gladden the human heart.
>   (Ps. 104:14—15a)

The entire psalm reflects the beauty and interrelatedness of creation and the relationship that creatures have with one another, and, most especially, with God as the creator of all (see, e.g., vv. 27—30).

In summary, Genesis 1—2, illumined by Psalm 104, today calls people everywhere to recognize the relationship that humans have with the rest of creation—that the human community is part of the grand picture of biodiversity, which has not only a common origin but also a common identity: it is "good"; it is "very good." Furthermore, Genesis 1—2 calls the human community to exercise "dominion" for all life in a way that celebrates creation's intrinsic goodness. To do so is to employ what it means to be made "in [God's] image, according to [God's] likeness" (Gen. 1:26), as understood by the early Jewish writers of the biblical text. This exercise of dominion is no longer something to be done as the fulfillment of a desire to be "godly"; it is the fundamental ethical responsibility of the entire human community today if patterns of injustice are to be broken and new ways of sustaining all life forms are to be learned.

This discussion on the need for the human community to recognize the intrinsic goodness of all life and to exercise dominion as an ethical responsibility leads back to the central theme of this chapter: hospitality of heart as a motivating principle of justice. Although this theme runs through many Old Testament stories,[8] it can be heard most practically, perhaps, in the following New Testament passages selected from the gospels, the writings of Paul, and other apostolic letters of the first century C.E. These stories focus on one aspect of justice—specifically, social justice—but contemporary theological reflection allows their message to be heard in a broader cosmological context.

Matthew 25:31–46: "...just as you did it to one of the least of these..." (v. 40)

Matthew 25:31–46 is a story within a narrative discourse aimed at teaching a lesson about the "end times." This passage is part of a larger literary unit that develops this Matthean theme of the *parousia* (see Mt. 24:3—25:46). In Matthew 25:31–46, Matthew depicts Jesus telling the disciples a story meant to respond to their questions about Jesus' coming and the coming of the end of the age (24:3). The passage opens on a metaphorical level (vv. 31–33) and then shifts to a parabolic level (vv. 34–46). The story that Jesus presents to his disciples puts forth a clear message: divine inheritance belongs to those who have shown concern for others, particularly concern for the poor and the outcast (vv. 34–46).

In Jesus' teaching, there is one main character, a king, and two groups: those who are seated at the king's right hand and those who are seated at the king's left hand. Symbolically, the story is about the judgment of the nations. The dualism that is part of the fabric of the story, as well as the references to the eternal fire, the devil and his angels, and eternal punishment

(vv. 41, 46), all reflect the culture of first-century Judaism that was shaped by Hellenism and apocalypticism, both of which, in turn, influenced and shaped the theological perspectives and beliefs of the Matthean community and those of the text's writers and later redactors and editors.

For Matthew's listeners, for Jesus' listeners, and for readers and listeners today, however, what is to be noted in this passage is the call to ethical praxis that begins with a hospitality of heart that welcomes and responds to those in need. Following verses 31–33, the narrative setting and opening action of the story, verses 34–36 describe the king offering a reward to those who have exercised hospitality and justice to him when he was in dire straights. What follows are three questions that express befuddlement on the part of those being rewarded by the king:

> Then the righteous will answer him, "Lord, when was it that we saw you hungry and gave you food, or thirsty and gave you something to drink? And when was it that we saw you a stranger and welcomed you, or naked and gave you clothing? And when was it that we saw you sick or in prison and visited you?" (vv. 37–39)

The king's comment to them drives home the message:

> "Truly I tell you, just as you did it to one of the least of these who are members of my family, you did it to me" (v. 40).[9]

The message delivered to those seated to the king's left is far from complimentary, and it points up that group's lack of hospitality and justice, which, according to the text, will lead to an unpleasant end.

Matthew 25:31–46 offers contemporary readers and believers a challenge—namely, to recognize that the pain and suffering of one person is connected to the pain and suffering of countless, nameless others who are often "the least" among the members of the human community. Furthermore, divine favor rests not with those who ignore such pain and suffering but with those who extend themselves and work to alleviate it.

Viewing the text from the vantage point of a sociological perspective, I assert that it is no longer enough to feed the hungry, clothe the naked, care for the sick, and visit the imprisoned within the human community. Care and comfort must be given to both human and nonhuman life. The violence and injustice being done by various groups within the human community now affects both human and nonhuman life, and both experience pain and suffering. Furthermore, what is needed is an ethical vision not only capable of penetrating to the core of injustice but also capable of envisioning an ethical praxis that settles for nothing less than justice and righteousness for all creation. Theologian Jeffrey G. Sobosan once wrote:

> What is needed is an expansion of our ethical concerns and commitments. While we recognize, for example, that maliciously damaging another human being is wrong, we must extend this principle (even when at first we think it will be honored more in the breach than the keeping) to all living things. So too with such generally acknowledged norms as sheltering the homeless, feeding the hungry, caring for the sick. This task is not easy, but it is possible, and we must muffle in our spirits the sweet temptation to give up. With the Buddhist saint we must strive toward that point where we can say, "All that is alive is a part of me, and I am nothing save for them." This is something at a high pitch, beyond the concerns of formal religion, recognizing that non-human life includes not just the animals but God as well. For God too survives in our lives only when we protect and nourish our feelings for the divine.[10]

Such a vision calls people to a certain largeness of heart that is ready to embrace all. It also calls for a certain steadfastness of spirit that is stubborn enough not to give up on justice in the

54 Justice

face of discouragement and even failure. To those who possess such qualities, a message of consoling hope needs to be heard anew: "Come, you who are blessed...inherit the kingdom prepared for you from the foundation of the world" (adapted from Mt. 25:34).

Luke 14:7–14: "...invite the poor..."

Luke's story about a Pharisee's meal celebration continues the theme of hospitality as it relates to justice. It offers a radical perspective about table gatherings and challenges traditional views of hospitality. This passage consists of two units: (1) an instruction for guests (vv. 7–11) and (2) a lesson for hosts (vv. 12–14). The setting is the home of a leader of the Pharisees, who is hosting a great dinner on the Sabbath (Lk. 14:1). Jesus is one of the invited guests and, as such, watches how the other guests have chosen the places of honor at the table. This action sparks a response from him, and he proceeds to tell the guests a parable (vv. 8–11).

The central point that Jesus makes to the quests is that they should take the lowest place at the table and wait to be invited to take a place of honor, if they are invited to do so at all. An aphorism sums up this teaching: "For all who exalt themselves will be humbled, and those who humble themselves will be exalted" (v. 11).

The focus on the seating arrangement at a meal celebration draws attention to the social status and social stratification that existed in the first century C.E. Joel B. Green offers this observation:

> This was a world in which social status and social stratification were vital considerations in the structuring of life, with one's status based on the social estimation of one's relative honor—that is, on the perception of those around a person regarding his [or her] prestige. For example, where one sat (was assigned or allowed to sit) at a meal vis-à-vis the host was a public advertisement of one's status; as a consequence, the matter of seating

arrangements was carefully attended and; in this agonistic society one might presume to claim a more honorable seat with the hope that it (and the honor that went with it) might be granted.[11]

In this setting, then, Luke depicts Jesus indirectly challenging the social status and stratification of his day, which becomes more to the point in the second part of Luke's narrative (vv. 12–14).

Following his remarks to the guests, Jesus addresses his host with respect to the kinds of people whom he should be inviting to one of his luncheons or dinners:

> "When you give a luncheon or a dinner, do not invite your friends or your brothers or your relatives or rich neighbors, in case they may invite you in return, and you would repaid. But when you give a banquet, invite the poor, the crippled, the lame, and the blind. And you will be blessed, because they cannot repay you, for you will be repaid at the resurrection of the righteous." (vv. 12–14)

Commenting further on the social situation of the first century C.E., Green states:

> The powerful and privileged would not ordinarily think to invite the poor to their meals, for this would (1) possibly endanger the social status of the host; (2) be a wasted invitation that could not be reciprocated; and (3) ensue in embarrassment for the poor, who could not reciprocate and, therefore, would be required by social protocols to decline the invitation.[12]

In these verses, readers see Jesus calling for an attitude of hospitality that would go against the grain of his day. Host and guest would sit at the table together as equals without any recourse to social status or social stratification. Jesus' directive to the host—to one of the Pharisees' leaders—not only breaks down the attitude of classism but also challenges the lack of hospitality and the "who's in–who's out" mentality that often leads to discrimination, all of which is unjust. Furthermore, that such a directive is made to one of the Pharisees' leaders in the context of a meal being hosted by that person, suggesting that among this group of religious people were some who had little or no concern for others who would, perhaps, be considered by them as "less fortunate" is quite bold on the part of Jesus. In addition, verses 12–14 suggest ever so subtly that a broadening and deepening of one's understanding of hospitality could lead to the breakdown of various artificial boundaries that either directly or inadvertently cause discrimination along with possible choices that could reflect such an attitude.

Although a link between hospitality and justice could be made from Luke 14:12–14, a rereading of the text from the perspective of the poor, the crippled, the lame, and the blind offers another idea for further consideration. Some might say that the point made that these people cannot offer reciprocal hospitality to the Pharisee is an assumption on Luke's part, who has also made it an assumption on Jesus' part. Sharon H. Ringe notes that:

> Luke takes for granted the assumptions that all persons with physical disabilities are poor, and that hospitality is a matter of mutual obligation between social equals. On the contrary, even in Jesus' or Luke's day, there were probably lame or blind people who were economically well off due to their families' wealth. More important, Luke does not make what to modern hearers is an obvious point, that society has an obligation to make it possible for persons with disabilities to participate as valued and productive members of society. There is no more reason to assume, let alone to justify, their poverty than to justify the poverty of any other man, woman, or child.[13]

Ringe goes on to say, "These teachings [vv. 12–14] ignore the extraordinary generosity and hospitality of many people who are poor, which far surpass the carefully calculated reciprocal invitations assumed as the norm."[14]

Ringe's comments bring Luke's limited social context to light and open up another area for conversation—namely, the ethics of biblical interpretation. Luke 14:12–14 and Ringe's comments on it call contemporary readers of the biblical text to certain wariness against privileging either the author's view represented in the text or the text itself, which can do an injustice to certain groups of people just by the way the story is told. The hallmark of the biblical tradition has always been God's hearing and responding to the voice of the poor or lost or disenfranchised, the *anawim*. It will take a certain hospitality of heart on the part of contemporary readers to receive and then cut through the many voices heard in the biblical text—especially to hear the text from the perspective of the *anawim*, and thus do the text "justice" by way of new interpretation.

Matthew 5:43–48: Justice to One's Enemies

Perhaps no other text in Matthew's gospel is as challenging as 5:43–48, which calls listeners then and now to the daunting task of loving one's enemies. Matthew opens the passage with Jesus addressing his disciples by quoting a phrase from the Torah: "You have heard that it was said, 'You shall love your neighbor and hate your enemy'" (v. 43). In Leviticus 19:18, the command is, "Love your neighbor as yourself." Nowhere in the Old Testament is the charge to hate one's enemies. This seems to have been a popular interpretation of the law during Jesus' time,[15] an interpretation that Jesus reinterprets: "But I say to you, Love your enemies and pray for those who persecute you" (v. 44). The motivation and reason for such a deed is given in verse 45. This verse highlights a quality of divine love—namely, that it is available and extended to all people regardless of their deeds: "for he makes his sun rise on the evil and on the good, and sends rain on the righteous and on the unrighteous."

Verses 46–47 include a series of questions that call for a hospitality of heart that goes beyond loving and welcoming one's own. A divine command closes the passage: "Be perfect, therefore, as your heavenly Father is perfect" (v. 48). Here perfection is meant to be dynamic and not static: "to be 'perfect' is to respond to other people—even our enemies— with the kind of compassion and desire for the good that expresses the way God responds to the world."[16]

In summary, Matthew 5:43–48 provides readers with a teaching on the essence of the law. And here, we are shown how it is to be understood with respect to human relationships, in the context of the ways of God, who, in justice, graces both the "righteous" and the "unrighteous." Such grace calls for extraordinary hospitality of heart that has compassion and not retaliation as its guiding principle.

Romans 14:1–12: Welcome without Judging

Hospitality of heart as it relates to justice is one among many themes found in the writings of Paul, particularly in Romans 14:1–12, a passage that cautions against judging others. Part of a larger block of material (Rom. 14:1—15:13), Romans 14:1–12 opens with a double directive: "Welcome those who are weak in faith, but not for the purpose of quarreling over opinions" (v. 1). This theme of "welcomeness" reaches its climax and conclusion in Romans 15:7: "Welcome one another, therefore, just as Christ has welcomed you, for the glory of God."

Addressed to the Gentile Christians of Rome, the first part of Paul's message focuses on food and on the "weak," who most likely are the Jewish Christians of the Roman community.[17] Paul lays down some basic rules of hospitality as to how the Gentile Christians are to treat the Jewish Christians. He next makes the point of telling them that God indeed has welcomed this group, and then with a theatrical question, he admonishes them against passing judgment: "Who are you to pass judgment on servants of another?" (v. 4).

The notion of judgment continues in verses 5–6, but here it pertains to assessment. Paul addresses indirectly the scrupulosity of some with regard to the Sabbath and continues to comment on food. He preaches that all choices should be made with God in mind and not for the purposes of self-righteousness.

Verses 7–12 pick up on the idea of everything being done in relationship with God. Here Paul includes himself in what now has become a very personal message: "We do not live to ourselves, and we do not die to ourselves. If we live, we live to the Lord, and if we die, we die to the Lord; so then, whether we live or whether we die, we are the Lord's" (vv. 7–8).

Following this statement Paul confronts his listeners directly. His two questions give evidence that some Christians were passing judgment on one another and even acting hostile toward one another: "Why do you pass judgment on your brother or sister? Or you, why do you despise your brother or sister?" (v. 10).

The key point of Paul's preaching comes in verse 12: everyone is accountable to God, who will discern one's deeds, and, thus, it is not the place of people to pass judgment on one another.[18]

Romans 14:1–12 offers readers and listeners today, especially Christians, a sobering and heartening word. A spirit of "welcomeness"—a spirit of hospitality of heart—is to be the pervading spirit among all people regardless of one's choices in life. For those who have made choices contrary to the norm, this passage brings hope. For those who have sat in judgment of others because of their diverse choices, this passage brings a challenge. In light of Romans 14:1–12, welcoming one another without judgment becomes not only a gesture of hospitality but also a matter of justice.

Hebrews 13:1–2; 3 John 2–8; Philemon 8–22: Hospitality to Strangers and Slaves

Other New Testament writings that speak of hospitality are Hebrews 13:1–2 and 3 John 2–8. Hebrews 13:1–2 is one of several "announcements" that comprise Hebrews 13:1–19. This first announcement offers the early Christian community a word of encouragement (v. 1) that is followed by an ethical injunction (v. 2): "Let mutual love continue. Do not neglect to show hospitality to strangers, for by doing that some have entertained angels without knowing it."

The mention of entertaining angels is undoubtedly a reference to Genesis 18:1–8, the story about Abraham's experience of how he entertained, with great hospitality, three men and then found out that one of them was Yahweh. F.F. Bruce comments: "Among Jews and Gentiles alike hospitality to strangers ranked high as a virtue; it was, indeed, a religious obligation."[19]

Third John 2–8 echoes the themes of love and hospitality mentioned in Hebrews 13:1–2. In a personal letter addressed to Gaius, the writer commends Gaius for his hospitality, which was praised highly by a group of people who had experienced it and who, upon coming to visit the writer, had commented on it.[20]

Finally, in Philemon 8–22, Paul advocates for a slave named Onesimus. He ran away, and has been with Paul throughout Paul's captivity, but now needs to be returned to Philemon, his "master." Because of good relations that exist between Paul and Philemon, Paul encourages Philemon to welcome back Onesimus in a manner that would be commensurate with Philemon's greeting of Paul: "Welcome him as you would welcome me" (v. 17).

All three of these passages focus on hospitality as a virtue to be extended to others regardless of their status in life. To do so is to offer to another what is his or her just due.

Concluding Remarks

The ancient biblical writings of both the Jewish and early Christian communities of believers provide the human community today with an understanding of how a hospitality of heart can be the spirit behind justice. It is not enough that laws be established to try to ensure what the ancients would call "the good life." History attests that laws do get broken, laws eventually discriminate, and laws sometimes no longer work in a world whose changes and discoveries now outpace its ethics. The selected biblical passages in this chapter suggest to contemporary readers and believers that justice is more than a matter of laws, and even more than a virtue that should be practiced. Justice is a divine imperative that has as its goal the full flourishing of all creation. For the human community, this sense of justice begins with human beings recognizing the intrinsic goodness of all creation, with humankind as part of creation's biodiversity, and not as its dominant species. What follows next is for the human community to understand "right relationship" and dominion as respect and care for all that exists. Human dominion finds its example in God's dominion as described by the psalmist in Psalm 104. Finally, if justice is to operate on a higher level than the law itself, then it has to flow from a heart transformed that, having been changed from stone to flesh, is not only vulnerable but also receptive to the unanswered needs and unjust pain currently present in the creation. Such a heart can do nothing less than welcome everyone and everything into it as it works to confront injustice in the face of an ever-growing anguish that is becoming more and more pervasive for human and nonhuman life. Such a hospitality of heart demands a robust spirit, one that embodies the hope and vision of the divine promise

> For I am about to create new heavens
> and a new earth.
> (Isa. 65:17)

and one that works increasingly until all life can come to experience its intrinsic goodness and fullness.

CHAPTER 3

Women, Children, Slaves, and Donkeys
The Work of Justice

The ancient vision alluded to in chapter 2, of a new heaven and a new earth, which the prophet Isaiah held out to the people of his day, offered them a sense of hope, especially after they had experienced devastation in 587 B.C.E. at the hands of the Babylonians. The foreigners invaded their country and left their land ravaged, their homes destroyed, their temple and their holy city Jerusalem in ruins, and themselves exiled to Babylon and Egypt.

Isaiah's ancient vision continues to offer hope in the twenty-first century for all creatures living with the threat of realized extinction and the grace of emerging redemption. Suffering and death caused by injustice continues to coexist with efforts to undo the thongs of oppression's yoke. For the vision of Isaiah to become the enduring reality, the work of justice must prevail. Part of the task of justice involves working on behalf of those within the human community who are the most vulnerable to the inordinate use of power—namely, women and children. To be engaged in the work of justice is to walk in the ways of God and along the paths of an ancient people whose stories offer both insight and challenge.

Throughout the Old and New Testaments, justice emerges as a theme, a virtue, and an ethical practice. This chapter looks at selected passages that focus on justice in relation to three groups of people in the ancient world: women, children, and slaves/servants. The last part of the chapter's discussion draws attention to Numbers 22:22–35, the story of Balaam's donkey. These stories present another perspective on justice and invite readers to engage in further ethical reflection.

Justice for Women and Children

Genesis 21:8–12: Hagar and Ishmael Cast Out

The story of Hagar and Ishmael being sent away by Abraham at the request of his wife Sarah is poignant yet disturbing. The narrative opens with Abraham celebrating his son Isaac's weaning (21:8). The story's tension mounts in verses 9–10:

> But Sarah saw the son of Hagar the Egyptian, whom she had borne to Abraham, playing with her son Isaac. So she said to Abraham, "Cast out this slave woman with her son; for the son of this slave woman shall not inherit along with my son Isaac."

Sarah's demand causes Abraham great distress, because Ishmael is also his son (v. 11). God steps in only to push Abraham in the direction of Sarah's demand, but this prodding does not happen without God revealing to Abraham the divine plan in store for both Isaac and Ishmael (vv. 12–13). Verse 14 describes Abraham sending Hagar and Ishmael away with nothing more than some bread and a skin of water. In verses 9–14 readers see an assertive wife and a compliant husband and meet for the first time one of the Bible's first single parents.

Verses 15–19 draw the narrative to a climax. These verses describe Hagar's distress and God's compassion. Having run out of water, and not wanting to bear the sight of her child about to die, Hagar puts her son under a bush at a slight distance from herself and then weeps (vv. 15–16). Into the midst of this tragic situation comes God, who is said to have heard the voice of the boy, though the text makes no reference to Ishmael crying out (v. 17). Next, an angel of God appears to Hagar, consoles her, and provides for her a well from which she draws water for her son (v. 19). Verses 20–21 conclude the story and highlight Ishmael's later good fortune and skill: "God was with the boy, and he grew up; he lived in the wilderness, and became an expert with the bow. He lived in the wilderness of Paran; and his mother got a wife for him from the land of Egypt."

Of all the characters presented in this story, clearly Hagar and Ishmael are the ones treated most unjustly. On the authorial level, Hagar as a character in the narrative seems to bear the mark of the author's biases: she is described as "Hagar the Egyptian" (v. 9) or the "slave woman" (vv. 10, 12). Attention is drawn to no other character's ethnic background or social role, and when featured in conjunction with Sarah on the narrative level, Hagar comes into view as the character deserving of the least respect from Abraham; from Sarah, who herself refers to Hagar as a "slave woman"; and from the text's readers. Furthermore, readers see that Hagar and Ishmael lose their home because of what seems to be Sarah's prejudice against Ishmael (v. 9), her unresolved contempt for Hagar (Gen. 16:4–5), and Abraham's inability to do anything humanly possible about the situation because of God's command and the divine promise afforded to Isaac (vv. 12).

As the narrative progresses, readers see that divine assistance comes to Hagar and Ishmael only after both of them have been cast out by Abraham, only after Hagar's water supply runs out, and only after Ishmael's voice is heard by God. It is significant that in the text Hagar lifts up her voice and weeps (v. 16) and immediately after that the narrator comments "And God heard the voice of the boy"(v. 17a), followed by a comment pertaining to the "angel of God":

...and the angel of God called to Hagar from heaven, and said to her, "What troubles you, Hagar? Do not be afraid; for God has heard the voice of the boy where he is. Come, lift up the boy and hold him fast with your hand, for I will make a great nation of him." (vv. 17–18)

According to the text, an angel responds to Hagar's voice but God hears and responds to Ishmael's. Granted, Hagar's concern is for her son (vv. 15–16), and God does respond to her need by providing the well of water for him, but there is no mention of God's care similarly for her, except indirectly through the angel. Thus, Ishmael's voice seems to be more highly favored than Hagar's. Would that the text had mentioned God hearing Hagar's voice as well as Ishmael's voice, and that God was with Hagar as God was "with the boy" (v. 20).

In summary, Genesis 21:8–21 describes an unjust situation being brought, in the end, to justice, through divine intervention. God does hear the voice of, and responds to, the most vulnerable one socially in the story—namely, Ishmael; and God does intervene on Hagar's and Ishmael's behalf, on the behalf of a homeless woman and her young son who have been treated unjustly by another woman. However, this final gesture of justice on God's part does not obliterate God's earlier actions as portrayed by the text. Sarah, who told her husband to cast out Hagar and Ishmael, no longer welcomed them. Abraham, perhaps, would never have followed through on Sarah's demand except for the fact that divine authority—God—told him to do as his wife had ordered. Hagar appears as a pawn who ultimately receives a divine promise and care, but at whose expense and at what cost? The theme of justice in Genesis 21:8–21 is ripe for ongoing discussion.

Genesis 22:1–19: Abraham and Isaac

A second story that pertains to justice and the life of a child is Genesis 22:1–19, a narrative that describes the near-sacrifice of Isaac, "child of the covenant," by his father Abraham. The narrative opens with the text's narrator making a specific theological statement about the events about to unfold: "After these things God tested Abraham" (v. 1). What follows is a narrated series of events that describe Abraham preparing to sacrifice his son Isaac to God because, according to the text, that is what God had commanded Abraham to do and Abraham was acting accordingly (vv. 1b–8).[1]

In the second part of the narrative (vv. 9–14), Abraham builds an altar, lays the wood "in order" on it, binds his son Isaac, lays him on top of the wood (v. 9), and, just as his knife in his hand is about to be lowered to slaughter his child, a divine voice breaks forth: "'Abraham, Abraham!...Do not lay your hand on the boy or do anything to him; for now I know that you fear God, since you have not withheld your son, your only son, from me'" (v. 12).

The one speaking to Abraham is an angel who acts as a divine messenger. The reference to Abraham fearing God implies awe and great love, and not fright or consternation.[2] The reference to Isaac being Abraham's "only son" is curious, since Ishmael is also his son. Isaac, however, *is* the son of the covenant.

The third part of the narrative (vv. 15–18) is generally considered to be a later addition to the Abraham-Isaac story. In these verses, the narrator depicts an angel delivering another message from God in which Abraham is lauded for his willingness to comply with the former divine command. This willing spirit of Abraham sets him up as a model of "obedience" and affords him blessings for himself and his offspring, and, ultimately, gains him the life of his son. A ram instead of Isaac becomes the sacrificial offering (see v. 13).

Absent from this story is the voice of Abraham. Are readers to presume that there was no dialogue between God and Abraham when such an excruciating demand was made upon the father of a child? Indeed, other biblical characters are portrayed as having something to say when divine demands were placed on them, demands which they eventually accepted for the sake of a larger mission of justice.[3] Here, however, Abraham is silent, portrayed as submissive, and asked to do something by God that appears to be without any association to the larger picture of justice. On a theological level, and one that reflects Israel's historical and religious situation of the day, the text stresses the sovereignty of God at a time when idol worship was a common practice. Abraham's nonverbal and submissive obedience accents the theme of divine sovereignty. For contemporary readers, what must be kept in mind is that this view of God represents the author's understanding of God, a view that is culturally and socially conditioned and representative of the beliefs and needs of its day.

Just as Abraham remains silent in the face of a heart-wrenching request made upon him, so Isaac is made to appear oblivious to his father's intentions. This is evident in the boy's comment and question: "Isaac said to his father Abraham, 'Father!' And he said, 'Here I am, my son.' He said, 'The fire and the wood are here, but where is the lamb for a burnt offering?'" (v. 7).

Isaac asks this question after he had carried the wood to the place where the offering was to take place—the wood that his own father had placed on him (v. 6).

In the end, justice is reckoned to Abraham and especially to his son Isaac. God gives a further command to Abraham not to sacrifice Isaac and then provides a ram for the offering.

For contemporary readers, the theme of justice is an important one with respect to a rereading of the text. First, the notion of God "testing" Abraham needs to be understood in the context of the narrator's voice: the narrator interprets the events of the story as a divine test of faith, an interpretation in need of ongoing theological reflection and discussion. Second, how Abraham is portrayed as the obedient one of God, who, in turn, is rewarded because of his obedience and faith, needs to be understood in the context of the story's central message, which is meant to serve a specific purpose and teaching for its historical, cultural, and religious time. And third, God's second command to Abraham—specifically, not to kill his own son—sets the stage for a larger picture of sacrifice that evolves within the tradition that comes into full view in Micah 6:6–8, where the prophet makes clear that the kind of sacrifice that God wants is not the burnt offerings of animals *or* the firstborn, the fruit of one's body. Rather, what is required is that one act justly, love tenderly, and walk humbly with God. The norms for acting justly are spelled out in Isaiah 58:6–14, which links fasting, another type of sacrifice, to ethical practice. Thus, the sacrifice of the ram in Genesis 22:13 reflects an ancient cultic practice that, ultimately, God does not want, just as God does not want the sacrifice of a human being.

Finally, the Abraham-Isaac story and the vision of Micah and Isaiah come to fullness in the life of Jesus in the New Testament. Jesus' divine obedience is linked to his mission of liberation and salvation of all. Paradoxically, his acting justly, his loving tenderly, his walking humbly with his God, and his loosening the bonds of injustice and letting the oppressed go free cost him his life. Human beings crucified him on account of his teachings and ethical deeds. The mystery of the resurrection attests to God's ultimate will for Jesus life—a desire foreshadowed within the Abraham-Isaac story and one embodied by the mortal life of Isaac that finds its fulfillment not in Jesus' death, as viewed traditionally, but in Jesus' gift of eternal life.[4]

Exodus 1:8—2:10: Baby Moses and the Ingenuity and Assertiveness of the Hebrew and Egyptian Women

Perhaps no other story in the Pentateuch is as painful and, at the same time, as heartwarming and hopeful as Exodus 1:8—2:10, whose central characters—four Hebrew women and one Egyptian woman—decide to act justly with ingenuity, assertiveness, and compassion on behalf of baby boys, and then one baby boy in particular, destined to die because of social oppression stemming from one country's leader's fear of a loss of power and land "under" his governance. Heard in a contemporary context, the infancy narrative of Moses and its unfolding events are a story about one of the first "boat people" and God's plan of salvation achieved through liberation that begins with a group of ethnically diverse and politically astute women who defy what is expected of them and thus go on to become examples of justice for past and present generations.

The prelude to Exodus 2:1–10, the account of how Moses as a baby is saved from death, is Exodus 1:8–22, a narrative that describes the Israelites' oppression by the Pharaohs, the ruling bloodline of Egypt. Verses 8–14 describe the current Pharaoh's opposition to the Israelites, how the Egyptians dread them, and the tasks imposed on them by the Egyptian taskmasters whose goal was to break the backs, figuratively, of the Israelites so that they would not gain the power needed to overthrow the Egyptians and their Pharaoh. Verses 15–22 depict the king of Egypt issuing a verbal edict to the Hebrew midwives:

> The king of Egypt said to the Hebrew midwives, one of whom was named Shiphrah and the other Puah, "When you act as midwives to the Hebrew women, and see them on the birthstool, if it is a boy, kill him; but if it is a girl, she shall live." But the midwives feared God; they did not do as the king of Egypt commanded them, but they let the boys live. So the king of Egypt summoned the midwives and said to them, "Why have you done this, and allowed the boys to live?" The midwives said to Pharaoh, "Because the Hebrew women are not like the Egyptian women; for they are vigorous and give birth before the midwife comes to them." So God dealt well with the midwives; and the people multiplied and became very strong. And because the midwives feared God, he gave them families. Then Pharaoh commanded all his people, "Every boy that is born to the Hebrews you shall throw into the Nile, but you shall let every girl live."

The two Hebrew midwives, Shiphrah and Puah, are clever in their response to the Pharaoh. This response both incites Pharaoh to call for further action and foreshadows the ingenuity of two other Hebrew women, Moses' mother and his sister.

Fearing for the life of her infant son, Moses' mother hides her little one in a papyrus basket that she seals and then puts among the reeds on the bank of the Nile River (Ex. 2:1–3). Moses' sister, later identified as Miriam, watches to see what will happen to him (Ex. 2:4). As the story unfolds, readers learn that Pharaoh's daughter discovers the basket, identifies the crying child in it as one of the Hebrews' babies, has pity on the little one, takes him as her own, agrees to have another woman (Moses' mother) nurse the child at the suggestion of Moses' sister, and then names the child (Ex. 2:5–10).

If Moses' mother had not fashioned the life-preserving basket and had not taken a chance with her baby son's life, and if Moses' older sister had not been as diligent and as clever as she was, and if Pharaoh's daughter had not listened to her heart and allowed herself to feel pity for the crying baby, and had not the courage to go against her father's edict, then Moses almost surely would have died. Salvation history for the Jewish people as we know it may not have happened through Moses.

Exodus 1:8—2:10 illustrates several points. First, justice is not always arrived at through a strict adherence to a law, especially when the law itself is not just. Second, women of diverse ethnic and religious backgrounds had an important part in the overall divine plan of salvation. Third, the divine plan of salvation transcends ethnic differences. Fourth, risk, compassion, and creativity are at the heart of the preservation of life, all of which leads to a fuller understanding of justice. For readers today, a "just" reading of this narrative would be one that celebrates the prominent place of women in salvation history and acknowledges ethnic diversity as part of that history and plan of salvation.

2 Kings 4:1–7: A Widow and Her Children

Another story that features a woman's assertiveness on behalf of her children and the justice they receive as their due is the tale about Elisha and a widow's oil. This narrative is part of a series of what have been labeled "miracle stories" in 2 Kings 4.[5] The socioeconomic situation precipitates the events that take place in this narrative. The woman is a widow, a mother of two children, and a member of the community of prophets. Her husband was a servant to the prophet Elisha. Economically, the woman is poor and in debt. Because of her social and economic situation, her children face the threat of slavery. In the ancient world, slavery could alleviate a debt and, in fact, it was part of the Hebrew legal system (see, e.g., Ex. 21:7 and Deut. 15:12). These circumstances lead the woman to appeal to Elisha the prophet for help.

The miracle of the flowing oil and borrowed vessels takes place under the direction of Elisha, but independent of his presence. The story concludes with the woman having enough oil to pay her debts, without having to give her children over to slavery.

Looking at the story as a whole, Terence Fretheim points out, "Elisha is a model of approach to needy people... He responds openly to her, carefully draws her out and allows her to express her need, starts with what she has and can contribute, specifies a procedure to be followed, and gives minimal instructions for following through."[6] He adds, "economic realities do affect 'family values.'"[7] Claudia V. Camp expounds on Fretheim's points and adds that the concerns addressed in this narrative are "real-life concerns of struggling peasants whose lot was made all the worse by unprincipled creditors and landholders. The miracle story thus also communicates the values of the just society promoted by the prophets of Yahweh."[8] Because of the values of a just society—values upheld by a male prophet—a woman and her children are able to enjoy life together as a family, free of debt and threat. Would that such justice and values be found among communities today, especially where there are similar economic situations in single parent homes. Yesterday's struggles as represented by this narrative remain ever-present today across the globe, with more than half the human population at the poverty level or below it. The need for justice calls out for a prophetic response.

Mark 5:21–43: Two Women Healed

Picking up on the theme of justice for women and children, the gospel of Mark presents two intertwined stories about a woman and a young girl who are restored to health and the fullness of life through Jesus. Common to both stories is a focus on the power of faith.

The first story centers on one of the leaders of the synagogue, Jairus, who, upon meeting Jesus, begs him to come and lay hands on his dying little daughter (vv. 22–23). Jesus' response is positive: he sets out with Jairus and goes to the little girl, only to be followed by a large crowd (v. 24). Within the crowd is a woman who has been suffering from hemorrhages for twelve years, who believes in her heart that if she touches Jesus' clothes, she will be made well (vv. 25–28).

The fact that the woman has endured much under many physicians suggests that she once had a substantial economic means, but is now destitute because her illness forced her to spend all that she had (v. 26). Instead of getting better, her physical condition has grown worse, which had social ramifications. Mary Ann Tolbert notes:

> In the Jewish context, her bleeding placed her in a state of perpetual cultic impurity (see Lev. 15:25–30) that would not only have prevented her from participating in cultic activities but would also have infected anyone who touched her, lay on a bed in which she had slept, or sat on a chair she had vacated.[9]

Tolbert comments further that:

> In a Greco-Roman social context, her appearance in public without companions may have indicated a "shamed" status, but the only explanation given by the Gospel is her disease. Her illness, then, has placed her outside the religious community and perhaps also outside the honorable human community.[10]

This woman is healed when she touches Jesus' clothes, and, aware that power had gone out of him, Jesus asks and discovers who touched him and remarks, "Daughter, your faith has made you well; go in peace, and be healed of your disease" (v. 34). The woman's initiative and faith, coupled by Jesus' receptive spirit to one in need, resulted in her being liberated from an oppressive illness and thus restored socially to her community.

Meanwhile, it is reported to Jairus that his little daughter, who had been on death's doorstep, has died (v. 35). Jesus encourages Jairus to keep on believing. The story ends with Jesus raising the little one from the dead, to the amazement of her family and those who were gathered with Jesus in her room (vv. 37–43).

The pleas of a father for his young daughter and the hope of a woman expressed so subtly did not go unheard or unanswered. Jesus responded. These two stories in Mark's gospel offer contemporary readers a challenge. While one may not be able to perform the divine deeds of Jesus for someone in need, it is within one's power to respond to a person in need. To do so is to embody the virtue of justice in a godly way, especially when one's response is on behalf of the most vulnerable, which, in Jesus' day, included women and children.

Mark 9:14–29: A Boy Healed

The theme of faith and care for children who are powerless against certain forces operative in their lives continues in Mark 9:14–29, a story about a boy possessed by a life-threatening spirit. From the midst of a crowd comes the voice of a father who has brought his son to Jesus to be freed from the possession of a spirit that has been affecting his son adversely (vv. 18, 22). Jesus' disciples have been unsuccessful in exorcising the spirit from the boy (v. 18). After Jesus upbraids those gathered for their faithlessness, he observes the boy's reaction to the spirit, and gathers more information from the boy's father, who pleads with Jesus for help: "…but if you are able to do anything, have pity on us and help us" (v. 22). Jesus responds curtly, "If you are able!—All things can be done for one who believes" (v. 23). The boy's father then blurts out, "I believe; help my unbelief!" (v. 24), after which Jesus rebukes the unclean spirit within the boy, commands it to depart from him—which it does—and then informs his bewildered disciples that this sort of work could only be accomplished through prayer (vv. 28–29).

In this narrative, Mark features Jesus responding to the pleas of a father on behalf of his son, who is victimized and possessed by a debilitating power, a force greater than himself. The unclean spirit has robbed the boy unjustly of a certain quality of life, and has even attempted to kill him. Jesus' response is an act of justice—he works to liberate the boy from the possession and oppression of the unclean spirit, while challenging and bolstering the faith of the crowd, the boy's father, and his disciples. This story suggests a link between justice and liberation: to exercise justice is to work to set others free from whatever may be compromising, oppressing, or endangering the gift of life. The story also points out the great care and concern that Jesus had for the well-being of children in the ancient world, which, when read in a contemporary social context, invites further ethical reflection on the quality of children's lives worldwide and the role that adults have as their advocates.

Luke 18:15–17: Jesus Welcomes the Children

Luke 18:15–17 is a fitting story to close this section on the Old and New Testament narratives that highlight children (and women) of the various communities. Luke opens his account with a comment that provides a setting for the action and lesson that follow: "People were bringing even infants to him that he might touch them; and when the disciples saw it, they sternly ordered them not to do it" (v. 15). Luke next introduces the character of Jesus into the story, whom he has oppose the disciples' order with the statement, "Let the little children come to me, and do not stop them; for it is to such as these that the kingdom of God belongs. Truly I tell you, whoever does not receive the kingdom of God as a little child will never enter it" (vv. 16–17).

Jesus' words extend hospitality to the children while teaching the disciples a stern lesson about the kingdom of God.

With regard to justice afforded to a community's most vulnerable human beings—infants and children—Joel B. Green offers several historical and cultural insights. First, Green points out, "Luke's phrase 'even infants' draws attention to the particular vulnerability of the smallest children, perhaps accounting for the widespread practice of infanticide and child abandonment"[11] Second, with respect to the phrase "little children" in verse 16, Green argues:

> [It] translates a term used for household slaves and children, those maintained in a relationship of subordination in a Greco-Roman household. Against this cultural horizon, the response of the disciples is easily understood, even justifiable. Why should Jesus' time be taken up with persons of such little importance, especially when a "ruler" was waiting in the wings (v. 18)?[12]

Green makes a third point:

> "Receiving little children" is tantamount to granting them hospitality, performing for them actions (washing of feet, kiss of greeting, and anointing the head—7:44–46) normally reserved for those of equal or higher status. That is, Jesus is asking his followers to embrace a topsy-turvy system of values and to extend respectful service to that social group most often overlooked.[13]

Green's final comment on the passage as a whole underscores the lesson that the disciples need to learn and opens the story up for further reflection:

> Failing to understand how the inbreaking kingdom undermines and supplants conventional canons of honor and status, the disciples fail to grasp God's

concern for those held in lowest regard, fail to comport themselves with humility so as to share that concern, and fail to function as Jesus' agents. Having refused to extend respectful service to the socially marginalized, having misconstrued the nature of the kingdom, how will they ever enter it?[14]

In this story, Jesus' disciples learn a powerful lesson, and, through the story, Luke calls his community to a deeper understanding of hospitality and justice as virtues that must be extended even to those on the lowest rung of the social ladder. The kingdom of God is not based on status and power, and, therefore, children and women who often had no status or power were among the ones most welcome by God.

Luke's story reminds readers and listeners today that, in God's home, all are welcome regardless of gender or status, and that if people are to be about the work of helping to bring the reign of God to its fullness, then they must extend a spirit of hospitality and act justly toward all people, especially toward women and children and toward those most vulnerable, the disenfranchised.

Justice for Slaves

The possession of slaves was part of ancient Israel's social, cultural, and economic life. At first glance, slavery appears to be unethical and inhumane, but before such a value judgment can be articulated, it is necessary to understand slavery in its social, economic, and historical setting. J. Gerald Janzen points out, "In the ancient world, one could become a slave through poverty, debt, capture in war, abandonment as a child, kidnap, or punishment for a crime."[15] J. Phillip Hyatt develops Janzen's point further and states:

> Among the ancient Israelites a person might sell himself or his wife or children into slavery because of poverty or specifically for non-payment of debt (2 Kings 4:1, Neh. 5: 1–5; Am. 2:6; the case of enslavement for inability

to pay the restitution required). Most slaves were apparently defaulting debtors, and probably served as domestic workers. The slave was considered as a chattel, the property of his owner, but it was also recognized that as a human being he had certain rights.[16]

Because slavery became an acceptable social institution, the Israelite community established laws in an attempt to assure fair treatment of those slaves associated with the community and to make provisions for their well-being. One set of laws governing the treatment of slaves can be found in Exodus 21:1–11, 20–21, 26–27.

Exodus 21:1–11, 20–21, 26–27: Servitude, Freedom, Justice

This particular passage in the book of Exodus outlines how the Israelites are to treat their slaves. The passage deals with two types of slaves: a Hebrew male slave sold into slavery (vv. 2–6) and a Hebrew daughter whom her father sells into slavery (vv. 7–11). The reasons why these two types of people are sold into slavery are absent from the text. One could hypothesize that the Hebrew male was the bargain to pay off a debt, and the Hebrew female was given over by her father because he could not provide for her dowry.[17]

The first part of Exodus 21:1—11 concerns laws pertaining to a Hebrew male slave (vv. 2—6). The section opens with God giving Moses an initial directive: "When you buy a male Hebrew slave, he shall serve six years, but in the seventh he shall go out a free person, without debt" (v. 2). The text indicates that enslavement was not a permanent state. The six-year term requirement lengthens the time specified in the Code of Hammurabi (117) by three years. Often, a slave was married, and, if so, then he and his wife were to be released together at the appointed time (v. 3). The directive in verse 4 safeguards the rights of the slave owner: "If his master gives him a wife and she bears him sons or daughters, the wife and the children shall be her master's and he shall go out alone." Those born in slavery were known as "homeborn slaves" (see Gen. 17:12, 27; Lev. 22:11; and Jer. 2:14).

Verses 5–6 focus on permanent slaves, which is a state chosen by the slave him- or herself, and not a status imposed by the slave owner. Hyatt observes, "Many a slave must have preferred permanent slavery with his family than to be separated from them, and also to face the possibility of destitution even though he was free."[18] The ritual described in verse 6 is alluded to elsewhere only in Deuteronomy 15:17. Janzen suggests that the ear piercing may have a double significance:

> First, the ear is the organ of hearing and obedience. As bored into the door(post), it attaches the slave's obedience to the master's house at the point through which he will daily go out to work and return to rest. Second, the word *elohim* [God] in verse 6 may refer not to God or "the judges" (NRSV note) but to household figures of deceased ancestors. Such symbolism suggests that the slave is being incorporated into the larger family. In the case of the female slave, she cannot be deprived of conjugal rights to proper care and respect. Otherwise, she is to be given her freedom, presumably to seek a more secure domestic arrangement.[19]

In sum, verses 2–6 describe laws for male slaves, a law that protects a slave owner, and a ritual that is to take place when a male slave chooses to become a permanent slave.

Verses 7–11 center on laws pertaining to female slaves. Treatment of a female slave differed from that of a male slave:

> A female slave...was treated differently, for she was normally expected to become the wife or concubine of the master. He might do one of three things with a female slave: (i) take her for himself; (ii) give her to his son as wife; or (iii) let her be redeemed, presumably by her own family. Provision was made that if he took a second wife, he must not diminish food, clothing and

conjugal rights of the first. If he did so she could go free without compensation.[20]

The legal material presented in verses 7–11 reflects the Israelite community's concern for female slaves and an attempt to safeguard them from becoming their owners' prostitutes.

Verses 20–21 deal with the legal ramifications of physical harm done to a slave by the slave's master. The context of the verses begs for ethical reflection: "When a slave owner strikes a male or female slave with a rod and the slave dies immediately, the owner shall be punished. But if the slave survives a day or two, there is no punishment; for the slave is the owner's property" (vv. 20–21).

These two verses drive home the reality that slaves were indeed another's property and, as "property," they remained vulnerable to the whims of their owners, whether they be kind or brutal. Verses 20–21 describe a situation of physical abuse. In the incidents that the biblical writer describes in verses 20–21, the slave is the object and recipient of another's brutal force. However, only if the slave dies immediately after being struck are there grounds for punishing the abusive slave owner. Although verse 20 hints at some sort of "chastisement" of the slave owner, the legal system described in the two verses clearly privileges the powerful and not the vulnerable. If the slave lives, the slave owner receives no corrective; if the slave dies, the slave owner does stand to be corrected, but only *after* the slave has died. For contemporary readers with a sensibility for justice, these verses are disconcerting. For those working on behalf of the vulnerable within any community, verses 20–21 could incite rage at an ancient legal system whose preferential option for those in power is, at times, still seen and felt today.

Verses 26–27 conclude this section on laws concerning slaves. Although the verses speak of liberation for slaves, freedom comes only after the slaves have endured physical brutality by their owners:

When a slave owner strikes the eye of a male or female slave, destroying it, the owner shall let the slave go, a free person, to compensate for the eye. If the owner knocks out a tooth of a male or female slave, the slave shall be let go, a free person, to compensate for the tooth.

Commentators note that these two verses are concerned with social justice for slaves. Hyatt observes that verses 26–27 are a "humanitarian law which has no effective parallel in the Code of Hammurabi."[21] Furthermore, Terence E. Fretheim adds, "Much of the segment of 21:1–32 is also concerned with social justice. The slavery materials (21:1–11, 20–21, 26–27) provide some protection for slaves from long-term servitude and inhumane treatment."[22] While the release of slaves by their owners after the slaves have had an eye destroyed or a tooth knocked out may have been understood as a humanitarian gesture on the part of the slave owner, and may have been interpreted as an act of "social justice" toward a slave and compensation for wounds inflicted, the fact remains that, although now freed, the former slave has had to endure physical abuse. To that extent, the act of liberation could prevent the slave from experiencing ongoing abuse from his or her master, but such freedom could hardly be called a "humanitarian law" or an act of "social justice." To make such claims would be to put a positive spin on a situation whose underlying cause for liberation is inherently and profoundly unjust in the first place. In that regard, biblical commentators hold up for merit the secondary actions of a slave owner but fail to address the primary issues of injustice—namely, the physical violence done to slaves by their owners.

Thus, Exodus 21:1–11, 20–21, 26–27 serve as a reminder that even though laws are created to safeguard one's life and property, many laws that have been written in good faith and with great judiciousness are inherently flawed and in need of revision if the fullness of justice is to be exercised on behalf of all people regardless of their status.

Expanding the Borders of Justice

Although many of the stories within both the Old and New Testaments speak of the need for justice within the human community, this focus does not exclude the need for justice among the rest of creation. For example, biblical law makes provisions for human beings as well as for animals and the land. Divine justice, exercised as compassion, embraces all life. The Wisdom of Solomon reminds past and present readers and listeners that indeed God loves all things that exist and detests none of the things that have been divinely made. Furthermore, God's immortal spirit is in all things (Wis. 11:24–26). Ben Sirach's (Apocrypha) message offers further insight:

> The compassion for human beings is for their neighbors, but the compassion of the Lord is for every living thing.
> (Sir. 18:13)

One story in the Old Testament that expands the borders of justice is the tale of Balaam and his donkey in Numbers 22:22–35.

Numbers 22:22–35: A Donkey's Challenge

Following some initial irregularities in the fabric of the storyline,[23] the story of Balaam and the donkey opens with God at odds with Balaam because Balaam has decided to set out with the officials of Moab (v. 22). The plight of the donkey unravels in stages (vv. 22–23, v. 24, v. 25, and v. 26), with the angel of God as the antagonist in each stage. Frightened by the angel at three different intervals, the donkey turns off the road and goes into a field (v. 23); it scrapes against a wall, and scrapes Balaam's foot as well (v. 25), and lays down under Balaam (v. 27). Each time the donkey reacted Balaam struck it. The climax of the story occurs in verses 28–30.

Appealing to the artistic style of ancient folklore, the biblical writer gives the donkey a human voice with which to address its master. Accordingly, the donkey's ability to speak is ascribed to God's work. The dialogue between the donkey and Balaam is noteworthy:

> Then the LORD opened the mouth of the donkey, and it said to Balaam, "What have I done to you, that you have struck me these three times?" Balaam said to the donkey, "Because you have made a fool of me! I wish I had a sword in my hand! I would kill you right now!" But the donkey said to Balaam," Am I not your donkey, which you have ridden all your life to this day? Have I been in the habit of treating you this way?" And he said, "No."

The story concludes with Balaam being confronted further by the angel as to why he struck the donkey three times. From the angel he learns that the donkey's reactions saved his life. Balaam acknowledges that he has sinned, for he did not know that the angel was standing in the road to thwart his travels. Chastened, Balaam continues on his journey with the officials of Moab, having been commanded to speak only that which comes to him from God (vv. 31–35).

Other than Genesis 3:1–24, nowhere else in the Bible does an animal speak (other than in symbolic form, such as the Lamb in Revelation). In both Genesis 3:1–24 and Numbers 22:22–35, the animals speak to human beings, one cleverly—the serpent—and one confrontationally—the donkey. Of significance in Numbers 22:22–35 is that the donkey speaks out against the injustice it has had to endure and directs its question squarely to Balaam: "What have I done to you, that you have struck me three times?" (v. 28). The donkey's second question highlights the relationship that exists between itself and Balaam: "Am I not your donkey, which you have ridden all your life to this day?" (v. 30a). The bond that the donkey feels toward Balaam and the faithful assistance it has provided for Balaam throughout his lifetime makes Balaam's treatment of the donkey all the more egregious. The donkey's third and final question finally evokes a response from his owner: "Have I been in the habit of treating you this way?" to which the owner replies, "No." (v. 30b). Balaam has done violence to his donkey and has violated right relationship. The fact that he can later admit that he has sinned is a sign of hope. Acknowledgment of one's transgression is the first step toward reconciliation.

The phrase "then the Lord opened the mouth of" used in Numbers 22:28 is also used in relation to God enabling a prophet to speak (cf. Ezek. 3:27; 33:22). Nonhuman life has confronted human life with regard to humanity's unjust ways. In today's world where many animals experience violence and cruelty at the hands of human beings, would that the animals again speak their prophetic word—their cry for justice—and would that the global human community respond as Balaam did—"I have sinned…" (v. 34). The donkey's final rhetorical question remains ever-pressing.[24]

Concluding Remarks

The global community has experienced great advances in education, technology, science, and political and religious affairs; yet one thing remains constant: suffering. Whether it be the struggles of a single parent, the hardships that children have to bear, a destitute widowed mother, infirmities of every sort that strike all generations, slavery—now in the form of human trafficking—or the abuse and violence endured by earth's nonhuman creatures, the cry of the poor is ever-persistent, as the selected stories in this chapter reveal. The work of justice remains central to the biblical tradition and its vision for life, and God's people are called to respond accordingly.

To respond to the cry of the poor and afflicted is to be and act godly. To work for justice on behalf of one's neighbor, especially on behalf of the least of one's brothers and sisters, is to embrace concretely one's God-given vocation that is intricately connected to one's having been created "in [God's] image, according to [God's] likeness" (Gen. 1:26). Brian Patrick offers a re-visioning of who our neighbor is:

Who is our neighbor: the Samaritan? The outcast? The enemy? Yes, yes, of course. But it is also the whale, the dolphin, and the rainforest. Our neighbor is the entire community of life, the entire universe. We must love it all as our self.[25]

Such a breath of vision and its challenge eloquently rereads the spirit of Torah that calls for love of God, love of self, and love of neighbor—particularly, the orphan, widow, stranger, and poor (see, e.g., Deut. 10:12ff; 14:28–29; 24:17, 18–21; Lev. 19:18).

The God of the Old Testament and the Jesus of the New Testament as portrayed in the biblical stories included in this chapter are actively engaged in the work of justice in and through the situations, circumstances, and people of the day. This work of justice and divine engagement in it continues in and through today's situations, circumstances, and people as well. Justice, rooted in love and exercised on behalf of another, reaches its depth and fullness when it is expressed as compassion, for compassion is not only the beginning and the end of justice, it is also the heart of justice.

CHAPTER 4

Compassion
The Heart of Justice

The medieval mystic Meister Eckhart once wrote:
You may call God love
you may call God goodness.
But the best name for God is
compassion.[1]

Eckhart also proclaimed, "The highest work of God is compassion."[2] In his book *The Mystic Heart,* contemporary spiritual writer Wayne Teasdale draws on the richness of the Hebrew noun *rahamin,* "compassion," which is understood as a divine quality, and *rahum,* "compassionate," a Hebrew adjective ascribed to God in the Old Testament. Teasdale writes:

> The divine...is infinite consciousness: the totality, the source, the spirit, the Tao, God, the ground of being, the ultimate reality, the ultimate mystery, the nameless one, Yahweh, Allah... This infinite awareness has a nature, an inner reality that expresses the unlimited mystery of the divine. The divine is boundless compassion in itself, and this quality governs its relation with all other

beings. This compassion is pure sensitivity, an eternal and total capacity to understand. Divine consciousness possesses complete understanding.[3]

Finally, expanding on Teasdale's concepts of compassion and understanding, Joan Chittister, noted author of spirituality, writes:

> Life is not perfect and people are not perfectible. Only understanding, only compassion—the ability to bear life with the rest of humanity, whatever burdens the bearing brings—perfects us. When that concept gets lost in the name of goodness, religion has gone awry and virtue has lost its meaning. God is compassionate and gives us what we need. No one can possibly be truly contemplative, truly in touch with the God-life, truly infused by the Spirit of God, who does anything less for the sake of the other.[4]

To return to the thought of Eckhart, then, we can now affirm his insight: "compassion means justice."[5] The biblical text offers many examples of the dialectic that exists between justice and compassion, and how compassion is the starting point, the heart, and the end of justice. This chapter looks at compassion in relation to transgression, compassion in relation to right relationship among all creation, and compassion as the motivation for acting justly and loving tenderly. As a virtue, compassion is a sign of new life and a testament to the presence of the reign of God.

The Interplay between Justice, Compassion, and Transgression

Genesis 3:1–24: The Garden Story and the First Sin

One of the most popular stories in Genesis 1—11, and one that continues to enjoy a rich history of interpretation is the story about Adam and Eve in the garden (3:1–24). Commanded by God not to eat of the fruit of a certain tree, both Adam and Eve do what they are not supposed to do (vv. 1–7). Their deed evokes a response from God, who enters into dialogue with the couple (vv. 8–13). Instead of accusing Adam and Eve outright, God asks them several questions aimed at disclosing the truth. By giving the sort of answers that they do, the couple indict themselves, and their sins of pride, failure to take responsibility, and disobedience become self-evident. Verses 14–19 describe the consequences that the serpent and couple will have to bear.

Comments by the narrator follow (vv. 20–21), the most important of which is verse 21: "And the LORD God made garments of skins for the man and for his wife, and clothed them."[6] At this juncture in the story, nakedness becomes associated with sin as well as the loss of innocence. Being naked caused Adam distress. The act of God clothing the couple in order to cover their nakedness can suggest that a person's sinful state is not permanent; God will continue to work with the human condition to transform it.

Verses 22–24 continue God's response to Adam and Eve on the occasion of their transgression. The final consequence that the couple will have to endure on account of their actions is expulsion from the garden.[7] Genesis 4:1 opens with the man "knowing" his wife Eve, who conceives and bears Cain.

In summary, Genesis 3:1–24 depicts God acting compassionately with justice in the face of transgression. The consequences for sin are meted out, and they are deserved. Yet the couple remains in God's favor and grace. God responds positively to a distressing situation, and the fact that Eve could conceive and bear life despite her transgression is a sign that neither she nor Adam have "fallen from grace" or out of divine favor. In the ancient world, the ability to bear children was a sign of God's blessing (Gen. 1:28) and divine favor (Gen. 29:31; cf. 1 Sam. 1:5–6; Hos. 9:14). Thus, the plight of Adam and Eve is a clear example of divine justice and compassion as a response to transgression, with compassion being the enduring virtue.

Genesis 4:1–16: A Brother Goes Astray

Following in his parents' footsteps, Cain also falls prey to sin. Genesis 4:1–16 describes the events that led up to and followed Abel's murder by his brother Cain. The crux of the story takes place in verses 9–15, which follow Abel's death (v. 8). Cain's transgression evokes a response from God, who, as in the case of Cain's parents' sin, does not immediately accuse Cain of the wrongdoing. Instead, God poses a question to Cain, hoping that Cain will take responsibility for action (v. 9a). Cain, however, offers an untruthful response, followed by a bold question of his own, addressed to God and rhetorical in nature: "Am I my brother's keeper?" (v. 9b). God confronts Cain again. The question and the statement are quite direct: "What have you done? Listen; your brother's blood is crying out to me from the ground!" (v. 10).

In verses 11–12, Cain learns of the consequences he will have to endure because of his transgression. In the face of divine justice, however, Cain does not keep silent. He makes his feelings known to God quite bluntly: "My punishment is greater than I can bear! Today you have driven me away from the soil, and I shall be hidden from your face; I shall be a fugitive and a wanderer on the earth, and anyone who meets me may kill me" (v. 14).

God's further response to Cain indicates a genuine concern for Cain despite his transgression. A mark on Cain, placed by God, will safeguard Cain's life. Ancient law required a life for a life. Cain's life, however, is spared and protected. Justice is served, but not without compassion.

Micah 7:18–20: A Prophet's Prayer

The themes of transgression and compassion come together in the poignant prayer of praise that the prophet Micah speaks to his God. Faced with the incredible iniquity of his people that eventually led to the downfall of the Northern Kingdom, with the Southern Kingdom following right behind the collapse of Israel, Micah never lost confidence in his God, whom he knew to be faithful and loyal. For Micah, God was ultimately a God of compassion whose final word and deed was not judgment but forgiveness. The poetic prayer of Micah calls us to remember:

> Who is a God like you, pardoning iniquity
> and passing over the transgression
> of the remnant of your possession?
> He does not retain his anger forever,
> because he delights in showing clemency.
> He will again have compassion upon us;
> he will tread our iniquities under foot.
> You will cast all our sins
> into the depths of the sea.
> You will show faithfulness to Jacob
> and unswerving loyalty to Abraham,
> as you have sworn to our ancestors
> from the days of old.
> (7:18–20)

God's anger in the face of iniquity and brutal injustice both within Israel and among the surrounding nations is righteous, but it is a passing emotion. Covenant relationship and divine compassion sprinkled with forgiveness—even without a hint of penitence on the people's part except for the prophet's intercession (Mic. 7:8–10)—is God's enduring gift.

Hosea 11:1–9: The Window to God's Heart

The prophet Hosea, a contemporary of Micah, also sings of a merciful God who remains compassionate toward the Israelites despite their infidelity, transgressions, and ingratitude. In Hosea 11:1–9, the prophet serves as God's spokesperson, delivering a heart-wrenching message of mixed emotion.

The rift between God and the people comes to the fore in verses 1–2. The God whose divine heart had been set on Israel, and who with great love freed the people from Egyptian bondage (Deut. 7:7–11), has been forsaken for other gods. In verses 3–4 the poet depicts God reflecting on what God had done for Israel in the past. How tender was the love. The tone shifts in verses 5–7. Because of their infidelity and iniquities, the people will suffer consequences that, according to the poet and biblical writer, God will cause to happen.[8] The tone shifts again in verses 8–9. The God of justice who metes out justice becomes sensitive to the movements of the heart and has a "change of heart":

> How can I give you up, Ephraim?
>   How can I hand you over, O Israel?
> How can I make you like Admah?
>   How can I treat you like Zeboiim?
> My heart recoils within me;
>   my compassion grows warm and tender.
> I will not execute my fierce anger;
>   I will not again destroy Ephraim;
> for I am God and no mortal,
>   the Holy One in your midst,
>   and I will not come in wrath.[9]
>   (11:8–9)

As verse 9 indicates, divine justice is not exercised punitively. God's justice is different from the exercise of human justice as prescribed by the law codes of the day. Thus, for both Micah and Hosea, God is a God of righteous anger who does not tolerate injustice. God's justice, however, does not flow from divine wrath; it flows from a heart filled with compassion born from the depths of struggling, faithful love.

John 7:53—8:11: Justice for an Adulterous Woman

Within the New Testament, we can also find examples of the interplay between transgression and compassion. One example is the story of the adulterous woman in John 7:53—8:11.

The setting for this story is the temple area, where Jesus is teaching those who had gathered around him. The scribes and Pharisees bring him a woman found guilty of adultery. Under Mosaic Law, justice for this crime demanded that both the man and the woman engaged in the sexual relationship be stoned to death (Lev. 20:10). Of note is the fact that only the woman stands accused; her partner is absent. Jesus deals directly with the scribes and the Pharisees' hostility toward the woman and himself. When he is finally alone with the woman, he addresses her in a manner similar to how God had addressed Adam, Eve, and Cain after their transgressions—he questions her: "Woman, where are they? Has no one condemned you?" (v. 10). Her reply is simple and candid, "No one, sir," and Jesus' reply is complementary: "Neither do I condemn you. Go your way, and from now on do not sin again" (v. 11). Like the God of the Old Testament who dealt with Adam, Eve, and Cain, Jesus does not condemn the woman, nor does he condemn the scribes and the Pharisees. His response to the woman's accusers is honest, just, and disarming; his response to the woman is compassionate. Strikingly, and unlike the God of the Old Testament, Jesus does not mete out consequences. He simply tells her to go away and not to sin again. With no further comment from either party, Jesus leaves the woman free to work out the details of her life. Clearly, this story exemplifies how justice and compassion are interrelated and ultimately liberating.[10]

Justice, Compassion, and Right Relationship

An ancient psalmist once sang:

The LORD is gracious and merciful,
  slow to anger and abounding in steadfast love.
The LORD is good to all,
  and his compassion is overall that he has made.
  (Ps. 145:8–9)

This passage sets the tone for the next section of this chapter, which looks at justice, compassion, and right relationship with all creation.

Within the Old Testament wisdom tradition, God's compassion becomes evident through God's dominion over all creation: everyone and everything receives their just due—i.e., what is needed so that life can flourish and be sustained. Psalm 104 is a song of praise that celebrates the beneficence of a just God whose compassion is for everything that has been created. The spirit of this psalm finds a home in the writings of the New Testament—in particular, Matthew 6:25–34, a story popularly referred to as "The Lilies of the Field." Part of the Sermon on the Mount discourse (Mt. 5—7), this passage is an instruction against greed and the hoarding of goods that is sometimes caused by anxiety, the passage's focal point. This story, however, is about much more. It speaks of God's compassion toward all of creation, and serves as a model for understanding right relationship.

Matthew's narrative depicts Jesus telling his listeners not to be anxious about what they need to live (v. 25). A comparison is then made to the birds of the air, the lilies of the field, and the grass of the field. Here Jesus asks the audience to consider God's care for birds and flowers (vv. 26, 30). In doing so, he drives home the point that the God of creation sustains and nurtures all of life regardless of need. This teaching about God's beneficence is meant to quell people's anxiety, focus them on the reign of God, and offer them some reassurance that indeed God will take care of them and provide for them. Finally, the story builds on various themes discussed earlier. To be made in God's image and according to God's likeness (Gen. 1:26–27) now calls the human community to exercise dominion, justice, and good governance on behalf of all life. To do so is to live compassionately and humbly with all that exists.

Luke 10:25–37: A Compassionate Samaritan

Perhaps one of the most popular stories in the New Testament is the parable of the good Samaritan (Lk. 10:25–37). It provides an eloquent instruction on love, compassion, justice, and right relationship.[11] The story opens with a lawyer questioning Jesus about what must be done to inherit eternal life. Jesus turns the question back on him, and the lawyer's allusion to Mosaic Law, specifically Leviticus 19:18 and Deuteronomy 6:5, provides a fitting response. The second half of the narrative depicts Jesus telling the lawyer a story about a Samaritan. The story serves to answer the lawyer's next question, "And who is my neighbor?"

Several characters play leading roles in Jesus' story. The cast includes a nameless man, some robbers, a priest, a Levite, a Samaritan, and an innkeeper. The narrative picks up pace when the unnamed man is accosted by the robbers, brutally harmed, and left half dead. Both a priest and a Levite see the man in peril but offer no assistance. They pass him by (vv. 31–32). Politically, the priest and the Levite represent the leadership of the people.[12] Religiously, they are restricted by the purity laws and regulations, which stipulated and limited contacts with others. The beaten man, probably bleeding, would have been considered "unclean." This is a classic example in which religious law and the keeping of it by two of its loyal followers have taken precedence over human need.

The third person to see the beaten man is a Samaritan who, upon drawing close to the man, is moved with pity (compassion in the original Greek) and reaches out to care for the beaten man's wounds. The Samaritan not only cares for the beaten man but also makes provision for his health care: he entrusts him to an innkeeper who is to watch over him and respond to his needs at the Samaritan's expense. The question Jesus addresses to the lawyer at the conclusion of the story frames the lawyer's initial question (v. 29). The lawyer comes to understand that "the one who showed him mercy"—the Samaritan—was neighbor to the suffering man. Jesus' further exhortation to the lawyer, "Go and do likewise," is pivotal: to be a good neighbor is to live a life of compassion, one that follows the way of the heart and not necessarily the outward principles of the law, and one that embraces and responds to "the other"—in this case, responding to a stranger—in the same way one would respond to a friend. Ironically, love for the stranger is stipulated in Jewish law (Deut. 10:19), a point that both the priest and Levite miss in their quest for personal holiness and righteousness.

The lawyer finally comes to grips with the point only after he has heard Jesus' message. Thus, in Luke 10:25–37, compassion becomes the bedrock for the exercise of justice, which, in turn, becomes the cornerstone for establishing "right relationship" whereby strangers become neighbors whom we are called to love, support, and sustain in the same way we love ourselves (Lk. 10:27).

Jesus: The Embodiment of Compassion

Matthew 9:35–38: A Crowd without a Leader

The gospel tradition bears witness that Jesus' whole life, mission, and ministry involved loving his "neighbors"—his friends, his enemies, and even people he did not know. In Matthew 9:35–38, Matthew teaches his listeners and readers that compassion was the motivation behind Jesus' reaching out to as many people as he did:

> Then Jesus went about all the cities and villages, teaching in their synagogues, and proclaiming the good news of the kingdom, and curing every disease and sickness. When he saw the crowds, he had compassion for them, because they were harassed and helpless, like sheep without a shepherd. (vv. 35–36)

Compassion was a quality of Jesus' character.[13] Thus, motivated by compassion, Jesus acted with justice on the people's behalf: he liberated them from many of their forms and experiences of oppression, whether it be sin, suffering, guilt, or infirmity.

Matthew 14:13–21 and 15:32–39: Food for the Multitudes

Compassion as the motivating spirit that moves Jesus to action is reflected in Matthew 14:13–21 and 15:32–39, two stories that depict Jesus surrounded by crowds of people. Matthew 14:13–21 tells us that Jesus had "compassion" on the crowd, cured the sick (v. 14), and then fed them. Matthew 15:32–39 captures Jesus' great sensitivity of heart: "I have compassion for the crowd, because they have been with me now for three days and have nothing to eat; and I do not want to send them away hungry, for they might faint on the way" (v. 32). The remainder of the story focuses on the multitudes being fed loaves and fish that Jesus blessed and the disciples distributed (vv. 33–39).

Because of Jesus' compassion, people whom he probably did not even know by name or acquaintance had their needs met. Those who were infirm were cured, and those who had spent days with him had their physical needs taken care of—they were fed and not sent away hungry. In this regard, justice, motivated by compassion, has been served. People have been relieved of present and potential suffering. Right relationship has been sustained, and the "strangers" among the crowds have become the "neighbors" whom, according to Matthew's gospel, Jesus has loved with great care.

Luke 7:11–17: A Widow's Grief Transformed

Compassion as the underlying motivation for justice also becomes evident in Luke's gospel, particularly in the story about the widow at Nain who lost her only son. The woman's situation is especially difficult because she is a widow, and her son who dies is her "only son." In the ancient world, if a woman lost her husband, then her care and inheritance would be entrusted to her son. In the event that she did not have a son, then the burden would shift to her husband's brother, and the Levirate Law would come into play (see Deut. 25:5–10; cf. Ex. 22:21–23).

Jesus, upon approaching the gate of the town, sees the dead man's body being carried out. He then encounters the man's grieving mother and has compassion for her. This heartfelt emotion evokes a response from him. He first offers the woman a word of comfort, "Do not weep" (v. 13), and then he raises her son—her only son—to life (vv. 14–15). Because Jesus' compassion motivates him to act, the woman is relieved of her grief, her broken-heartedness is healed, and her son is liberated from death and restored to life. Justice has been served, life flourishes, and the reign of God becomes apparent (vv. 16–17).[14]

Concluding Remarks

The various stories in this chapter have tried to provide an insight into the relationship between justice and compassion. It is possible to act justly and to afford another justice without feeling any sense of compassion, as in the case of the Lukan parable of the recalcitrant judge who grants a persistent widow justice because she continually bothers him (Lk. 18:1–8). If, however, one desires to live a life rooted in the Spirit of God and the Spirit of Jesus, then one's response to life—to creation—calls for a response that roots justice in something that is far deeper than what would be required by law. The selected Old and New Testament stories in this chapter celebrate God and Jesus as inherently relational[15] and in right relationship with all creation. The sustaining, life-giving energy that undergirds the relationship that the Divine has with all creation is abiding love. Such love pours itself out in compassion, whereby the life of everything and everyone that exists is respected, valued, cherished, and sustained. It is justice to the highest degree, reminding us that both the oppressed (Abel) and the oppressor (Cain) are made in God's image, according to God's likeness (Gen. 1:26).

Whenever anyone or anything suffers, God—whose immortal Spirit is in all things (Wis. 12:1)—suffers too. Suffering can take many forms, as we have seen in the stories included in this chapter and in other texts within the Bible as a whole. Because of God's steadfast love, the divine response to all of life and its many diverse situations will always be compassion—a compassion that renders justice and hospitality of heart to the saint and sinner alike, and to anyone or anything in need.[16] Neither accusatory, condemnatory, nor judgmental, justice that flows from compassion hopes for a change of heart, reconciliation, healing, and the full flourishing of life for all in peace. Such a vision is central to the Christian vocation, as Paul reminded the early Christians at Colossus:

> As God's chosen ones, holy and beloved, clothe yourselves with compassion, kindness, humility, meekness, and patience. Bear with one another and, if anyone has a complaint against another, forgive each other; just as the Lord has forgiven you, so you also must forgive. Above all, clothe yourselves with love, which binds everything together in perfect harmony. And let the peace of Christ rule in your hearts, to which indeed you were called in the one body.(Col. 3:12–15)

This vision is also central to the vocation of becoming fully "human"—fashioned in God's image, according to God's likeness. This means that we are called to be just in all our ways and kind in all our deeds, for, as the psalmist proclaimed ages ago:

> The LORD is just in all his ways,
> and kind in all his doings.
>   (Ps. 145:17)

Would that humankind come to understand the fullness to which we are called, and the responsibility we have toward all creation. God, whose love is steadfast and whose compassion is over all that has been made (Ps. 145:8–9), has entrusted us with creation.

CHAPTER 5

Peace

The Flower of Justice

The people of Israel understood covenant as relationship: relationship with God, relationship with one another, and relationship with the natural world—particularly with the land and animals. They also understood that Torah was not only Law but also an attitude and way of life meant to safeguard and sustain covenant relationship.[1] Following God's ways and observing God's statutes and ordinances was primarily for the purpose of enjoying the good life in an atmosphere of security: "You shall observe my statutes and faithfully keep my ordinances, so that you may live on the land securely. The land will yield its fruit, and you will eat your fill and live on it securely" (Lev. 25:18–19).

When Israel was in its greatest internal turmoil and living under the threat of invasion from Assyria, Hosea proclaimed an eschatological vision that offered the people a word of hope and a promise of covenant renewal on God's part. This renewed covenant would include God's relationship with the people, and the people's relationship with nonhuman life and the land. The fruit of this renewed covenant would be peace:

> On that day, says the Lord, you will call me, "My husband," and no longer will you call me, "My Baal." For I will remove the names of the Baals from her mouth, and they shall be mentioned by name no more. I will make for you a covenant on that day with the wild animals, the birds of the air, and the creeping things of the ground; and I will abolish the bow, the sword, and war from the land; and I will make you lie down in safety. And I will take you for my wife forever; I will take you for my wife in righteousness and in justice, in steadfast love, and in mercy. I will take you for my wife in faithfulness; and you shall know the Lord. (Hos. 2:16–20)

This theme of peace is echoed in Isaiah 2:2–4 and Micah 4:1–5, which both speak of swords being turned into plowshares, spears into pruning hooks, nations no longer lifting up swords against each other, and none of them learning war anymore. It is significant in the prophetic vision that God will be the one who will establish peace, and thus they wait for a spirit from on high to be poured out among them (Isa. 32:14–15). When this experience happens, then there will be abiding justice and righteousness in the land, the effect of which will bring peace (Isa. 32:16–17). According to the prophets, this vision of peace will be accomplished through a messianic leader who will govern the people with compassionate justice. Peace as the flower of justice blossoming through good governance is a theme found in the writings of the prophet Isaiah in the Old Testament that we often connect to Jesus as Messiah and the embodiment of the prophetic tradition.

A Prophetic Vision

Isaiah 9:1–7: The Promise of a Righteous Leader

Isaiah 9:1–7 celebrates the liberation of Israel from the oppressive experience of war. This liberation will be done by God through a new leader of Davidic lineage, born to the people in their midst. Historically, this new leader is probably Hezekiah,

Ahaz's successor, who began his reign either 725 or 715 B.C.E. Although this Isaian prophecy has an historical referent, it also has an eschatological dimension, pointing forward to other Isaian passages that are also messianic (Isa. 11:1–9; 42:1–4; and 61:1–4). This new leader envisioned by Isaiah and named "Wonderful Counselor," "Mighty God," "Everlasting Father," "Prince of Peace" (v. 6) will establish peace in the land and uphold it with justice and righteousness (v. 7).

Isaiah 11:1–9: The Vision of the Peaceful Kingdom

Isaiah 11:1–9 describes the qualities of the awaited messianic leader and the effects that the leader's good governance will have in the land. In verses 1–3, Isaiah proclaims that the new leader will be from the line of David (v. 1) who will not only be inspired by God (v. 2) but also in right relationship with God (v. 3a). This right relationship with God will effect how the leader will govern. In verses 3b–5, Isaiah describes how the leader will govern—namely, with righteousness, equity, nonviolence, and fidelity. The effect of just governance will be peace in the land. Isaiah's vision makes clear that, when justice is exercised on the part of leadership, there will be positive outcomes for all creation, both human and nonhuman, with new relationships being established within creation. Thus, Isaiah's ancient message has sharp implications for a socio-ecological vision of justice and peace.[2]

Isaiah 42:1–4: The Servant Leader and the Dawn of Peace

Later in Isaiah comes another description of the new leader. In Isaiah 42:1–4, , for the first time, this new envisioned leader is identified as God's "servant." This servant of God is the chosen one in whom God takes delight (v. 1a). Imbued with God's Spirit, the servant will bring forth justice to the nations (v. 1b). This "justice" to the nations will not be like the justice of the old world that is established through violence (see, e.g., Isa. 13—23 and Jer. 46—51). Rather, the justice to the nations will be the reestablishment of right relationship among themselves, with the presence of God in the midst (cf. Mic. 4:1–5 and Isa.

2:1–4). God's servant will do this persistently, faithfully, and nonviolently. This justice that the servant will faithfully bring forth and that will be established in the earth is peace (cf. Isa. 9:7). God's servant will embody a new way of establishing justice. As one who will bring about a new world order, the servant is him- or herself the embodiment of the new world order—namely, the incarnation of the reign of God and the peaceable kingdom (cf. Lk. 17:20–21).[3]

Isaiah 61:1–4: The Anointed One and the Time of Jubilee

Isaiah 61:1–4 is the final reference to the one chosen by God to bring about restoration. The focus of this passage is on the mission to be accomplished by the one empowered by the Spirit of God (cf. Isa. 11:2; 42:1). The anointed one in this passage participates actively in the ongoing divine vision of salvation.[4] Although this passage reflects historically the exile of the Judahites to Babylon, with the "captives" and "prisoners" likely referring to the Judahite exiles, when heard in an eschatological context, the passage presents "a concise summary of the mission of a servant of God in any age. It is a mission to raise up the lower strata of society. The Gospel of Luke has Jesus read this text, with minor variations, at the outset of his career (Lk. 4:17–19)," as John J. Collins has suggested.[5] The "year of the Lord's favor" refers not only to the sabbatical year (Lev. 25:1–7 and Deut. 15:1–18) but also to the year of the jubilee (Lev. 25:8–55), a time characterized by the cancellation of debts, and the return of people to their families and to their land—their inheritance—and the redemption of people from oppression. The anointed one of God will usher in a time of celebration and restoration, and, by extension, a time of peace.[6]

A Prophetic Reality

Matthew 12:15–21 and Luke 4:16–30: Jesus, the Embodiment of Isaiah's Vision

Two passages in the gospels bring to light the prophetic vision of Isaiah in new and expanded contexts: Matthew

12:15–21 and Luke 4:16–30. Matthew 12:15–21 presents the evangelist's understanding of Jesus' mission and ministry, which connects to Isaiah 42:1–4. Luke 4:16–30 presents the author's description of Jesus declaring his mission and ministry to those gathered in the synagogue. In reading from Isaiah 61:1–2, Jesus connects his mission and ministry to the anointed one in Isaiah 61:1–2. He omits, however, the reference to the day of vengeance of God, and then tells his audience, "Today this scripture has been fulfilled in your hearing" (Lk. 4:21).

Throughout the gospels, and in particular Luke's gospel, Jesus proclaims the year of the Lord's favor (Lk. 4:19) through the works that he does among all God's people. He liberates people from physical suffering (e.g., Lk. 5:12–16; 7:1–10), from death (e.g., Lk. 7:11–17), from being possessed by demons (e.g., Lk. 4:31–37; 8:26–39), from narrow interpretations of the Law (e.g., Lk. 6:1–5; 10:25–37), and, most especially, from sin (e.g., Lk. 5:17–26). In compassionately restoring people's lives, he brings them justice. In confronting the deeds of the Pharisees and lawyers (Lk. 11:37–53; cf. Mt. 23:1–36, especially v. 26), he offers "recovery of sight to the blind" to whose focus is on the written law that divides instead of on the law written within the heart that unites (see Jer. 31:31–34; cf. Mt. 22:34–40; Lk. 10:25–37). Jesus' whole mission and ministry was to proclaim the jubilee year, to restore people to right relationship with God and with one another, and to redeem them from the shackles of sin. He worked at these tasks up to the point of his death, and accomplished them through his death and resurrection, whereby, similar to the prophets before him, he interceded for God's people (cf. Hos. 6:1–3; Mic. 6:6–8), reconciling all to God forever through the divine gift of forgiveness and reconciliation (Lk. 23:34; cf. Col. 1:15—20). This was Jesus' greatest act of justice, accomplished through compassion and peace on his part. He did not demand the lives of his oppressors, and throughout his entire mission and ministry he worked for justice among all so that peace could take root and flourish within all and among all.

Perhaps one of the greatest works of justice for the sake of peace was Jesus' message to and work among the Gentiles. Matthew understands Jesus' mission to include proclaiming justice to the Gentiles (Mt. 12:18), bringing justice to victory (Mt. 12:20), and giving the Gentiles hope (Mt. 12:21; cf. Lk. 2:29–32). In the context of Matthew's world, a rift existed between the Jews and the Gentiles. Although Jesus' mission is focused primarily on "the lost sheep of the house of Israel" (Mt. 10:6), a Canaanite woman—a Gentile—challenges this focus and succeeds in enlarging his sense of mission and ministry (Mt. 15:21–28), thereby extending justice to the Gentiles. Jesus' reinterpretation of the Law, however, is what essentially gives them hope and brings them justice. No longer are they excluded from covenant relationship and salvation based on circumcision and the external practice of the Mosaic Law. Love, as the fulfillment of the Law and the prophets, opens the door for them (see Mt. 22:34–40). Right relationship, eclipsed in Deuteronomy 6:4–6 and 10:12—16 and proclaimed in Isaiah 56:1–8, provides the Gentiles with a place at the table, a place that some non-Gentiles would rather they not have. Jesus' mission and ministry to the Gentiles is limited in scope during his lifetime as viewed in the gospels. It reaches its climax and fullness, however, through Paul (see Rom. 11:13).

Both the Acts of the Apostles and the writings of Paul shed light on the divine activity within the lives of the Gentiles. They hear and receive the good news (Acts 10:34—43); are recipients of the Holy Spirit, to the surprise of circumcised believers (Acts 10:44–48); have also been given by God a spirit of repentance that leads to life (Acts 11:1–18); are destined for eternal life (Acts 13:44–52); have been favored by God (Acts 15:14); are the recipients of salvation (Rom. 11:11–24), fellow heirs, members of the same body; and are sharers in the promise in Christ Jesus through the gospel (Eph. 3:6). Thus, justice to the Gentiles and the recognition and celebration of it is a major movement toward unity in the first century C.E., and it is also a major movement toward the establishment of the reign of God brought forth through Christ and Christ's teaching. Christ, as the incarnation of God's love, offers hospitality of heart to all, thereby extending not only the gifts of reconciliation and unity but also peace. Paul's words to the Gentiles in Ephesians 2 add a fitting conclusion to the discussion at hand:

> So then, remember that at one time you Gentiles by birth, called "the uncircumcision" by those who are called "the circumcision"—a physical circumcision made in the flesh by human hands—remember that you were at that time without Christ, being aliens from the commonwealth of Israel, and strangers to the covenants of promise, having no hope and without God in the world. But now in Christ Jesus you who once were far off have been brought near by the blood of Christ. For he is our peace; in his flesh he has made both groups into one and has broken down the dividing wall, that is, the hostility between us. He has abolished the law with its commandments and ordinances, that he might create in himself one new humanity in place of the two, thus making peace, and might reconcile both groups to God in one body through the cross, thus putting to death that hostility through it. So he came and proclaimed peace to you who were far off and peace to those who were near; for through him both of us have access in one Spirit to the Father. So then you are no longer strangers and aliens, but you are citizens with the saints and also members of the household of God, built upon the foundation of the apostles and prophets, with Christ Jesus himself as the cornerstone. In him the whole structure is joined together and grows into a holy temple in the Lord; in whom you also are built together spiritually into a dwelling place for God. (Eph. 2:11–22)[7]

Concluding Remarks

In the mid 1960s, a popular bumper sticker read, "If you want peace, then work for justice." Peace is more than a feeling, an emotion, or an experience. Peace is the flower of justice. It is a divine gift meant for all creation and all communities of life within creation. Peace is the fruit of right relationship, and it is the work of God for God's people (Eph. 2:14). The Old Testament prophets, in particular Isaiah, make the links between justice and peace, and highlight the role of leadership in the mission and ministry of justice that leads to peace. The gospel writers, especially Matthew and Luke, offer a picture of Jesus as the embodiment of the messianic servant-leader heralded by the prophet Isaiah. Paul's preaching and writings disclose more fully the magnificent vision of God that was given in the writings of the Prophets and the gospels.

With respect to hearing the biblical text anew, these selected passages in this chapter call us today to reexamine our understanding of leadership, to challenge the goals that are on the agendas of many of the world's leaders, and to redefine our notions of justice, peace, right relationship, and the reign of God. The passages also call us to embrace more deeply, once again, our vocation as human beings who, having been created in God's image and according to God's likeness, are imbued with God's Spirit (Gen. 2:7). This Spirit is the same Spirit that was present at the time of creation (Gen. 1:1–2), is part of all creation (Wis. 12:1), and was present in the prophets of old (Mic. 3:8). This Spirit is messianic (Isa. 11:1–3; 42:1–4), was part of Jesus' understanding of himself and his mission (Mt. 12:18–21; Lk. 4:16–19), and has been poured out upon all flesh (Acts 2:17–18).

Finally, these texts invite all people to become the leaders they are meant to be, with everyone governing well and working for justice. The reign of God is in our midst, and the peaceable kingdom is God's prophetic dream for all creation. In the words of Rabbi Rami M. Shapiro:

It is up to us to receive and transmit our Torah,
it is up to us to see that the world still stands.
May the time be not distant
when nation will not lift up sword against nation,
neither shall they learn war any more.
They shall beat their swords into ploughshares,
for the earth will be filled with the wonder of life.
Then shall we sit under our vine and our fig tree
and none shall be afraid.[8]

"Would that we, yes we, would only recognize on this day the things that make for peace!" (adapted from Lk. 19:42).

EPILOGUE

Justice

An Invitation and a Vocation

U.S. Astronaut James Irwin, in his memoirs about his space travels, wrote:

> The Earth reminded us of a Christmas tree ornament hanging in the blackness of space. As we got farther and farther away it diminished in size. Finally it shrank to the size of a marble, the most beautiful marble you can imagine. That beautiful, warm, living object looked so fragile, so delicate, that if you touched it with a finger it would crumble and fall apart. Seeing this has to change a [person], has to make a [person] appreciate the creation of God and the love of God.[1]

So simply and yet so well, Irwin's reflection captures the reality of Earth and the reality of life on the planet. Our lives and, indeed, the life of the planet itself and every single species of life on the planet hang in the balance. Will the scales tip toward recovery and restoration or will they tip toward apathy and extinction? The planet is fragile…delicate. Life on the planet is fragile…delicate. The planet is on the verge of crumbling and falling apart because of social and environmental injustice that continues to erode its core, its heart. And justice is blind. Have we not been given, however, a share of the Spirit to proclaim recovery of sight to the blind? The coastlands wait for our teaching.

This volume has looked at the theme of justice in the Bible from a variety of perspectives and through several different lenses. It has called into question a vision of justice that celebrates liberation accomplished through violence. It has tried to show the interplay between justice, compassion, right relationship, and peace. When justice is rooted in something deeper than law, then justice has the potential for being transformative. The volume has also tried to show the interconnectedness between human and nonhuman suffering, the need for justice on behalf of all creation, and the hope and goodness of peaceful life that justice can usher forth if practiced through good governance. Finally, the volume has tried to redefine our understanding of who we are as human beings and in so doing has offered the human community the challenge to embrace our true identity and the responsibilities associated with that knowledge of self. Our world is sacramental, revelatory, and holy, but it is riddled with pain and suffering caused by unnecessary injustice. The reign of God is in our midst, and the vision of peace is within our grasp, if only everyone would heed the words of the ancient prophet Micah:

> [God] has told you, O mortal, what is good;
>   and what does the Lord require of you
> but to do justice, and to love kindness,
>   and to walk humbly with your God?
>   (Mic. 6:8)

Micah's words are simple; perhaps so simple that we fail to understand them. Justice begins with a humble walk with God, who will transform us on the way, while gracing us with the knowledge, strength, wisdom, and confidence we need to do what has to be done.

> "And you, child, will be called the prophet of the Most
> High;
> > for you will go before the Lord to prepare [God's]
> > ways,
> to give knowledge of salvation to [God's] people
> > by the forgiveness of their sins.
> By the tender mercy of our God,
> > the dawn from on high will break upon us,
> to give light to those who sit in darkness and in the
> > shadow of death,
> > to guide our feet into the way of peace."
> > (Lk. 1:76–79)

May the child within us all take that humble walk with God, and may we embrace the prophetic vocation that is ours.

Notes

Introduction

[1] See, e.g., Hos. 4:1–3; Isa. 5:8–13.
[2] See, e.g., Mic. 2:1–2, 8–9; 3:1–12; 7:1–6.
[3] Deut 7:7–11 implies that God had a particular relationship with Israel, but not to the exclusion of the other nations who also shared in God's divine favor and plan for universal salvation (see, e.g., Isa. 2:2–4; Mic. 4:1—5.)
[4] See, e.g., Gen. 18:19; Deut. 16:20; 24:17; 1 Kings 10:9; Isa. 1:17; 42:1–4; 56:1; Jer. 21:12; 22:3.
[5] See also Mt. 12:18, 20; Lk. 11:42.
[6] This understanding of mercy as justice understands not only the necessity of justice, but also the necessity that mercy be inseparable from justice and vice versa. See, e.g., Hos. 4:1–10 and 11:8–9; and especially Mic. 7:18–20.
[7] Cf. Mt. 5:44–45.
[8] See, e.g., Isa. 1:16–17; 56:1; Mt. 23:23; and Lk. 11:42.
[9] See, e.g., two recent works that explore the topic of justice: for the Bible as a whole, see Enrique Nardoni, *Rise Up, O Judge: A Study of Justice in the Biblical World*, trans. Sean Charles Martin (Peabody, Mass.: Hendrickson, 2004), and for the book of Isaiah in particular, see Thomas L. Leclerc, *Yahweh Is Exalted in Justice: Solidarity and Conflict in Isaiah* (Minneapolis: Fortress Press, 2001.)

Chapter 1: Justice and Liberation Attained through Violence

[1] For biblical references supporting the principle of *lex talionis*, see Ex. 21:23–25; Lev. 24:19–21; and Deut. 19:21. Clearly, the Mosaic Law Code supported this type of "justice" for offenses incurred.
[2] See, e.g., Isa. 55:7; Jer. 3:12, 14, 22; Hos. 6:1; 14:1; Mal. 3:7.
[3] See also Ezek. 33:17–20.
[4] See, e.g., Jer. 46:1—56:58; Ezek. 25:1—32:32; 36:1–7; Amos 1:2—2:3.
[5] See Deut. 7:7–11.
[6] For further discussion on the plagues and the plague tradition in the Old and New Testaments, see Carol J. Dempsey, "Plagues," in *The Collegeville Pastoral Dictionary of Biblical Theology*, ed. Dianne Bergant, CSA; Leslie Hoppe, OFM; Barbara Reid, OP; Carroll Stuhlmueller, CP, gen. ed.(Collegeville, Minn.: Liturgical Press, 1996), 739–41.
[7] In his commentary on Exodus, J. Philip Hyatt focuses on the question of the historicity of the first plague and outlines two common explanations for the Nile seemingly turning to blood: (1) "When the Nile begins to rise in June, it often has a dark reddish hue because of the presence in the water of red mud picked up by the river as it flows through the mountains of Abyssinia"; and (2) "the micro-organisms—flagellates, algae, or the like—which might be effective also in killing the Nile fish." See Hyatt, *Exodus* (Grand Rapids: Eerdmans, 1980), 107.
[8] It is possible to understand this plague as an attack on the Egyptian pantheon. One of Egypt's esteemed goddesses, Hekt, is represented by a frog. See Göran Larsson, *Bound for Freedom: The Book of Exodus in Jewish and Christian Traditions* (Peabody, Mass.: Hendrickson, 1999), 61.
[9] For a comprehensive understanding of the term "dust," see Gen. 3:19; Eccl. 3:20; Job 4:19; 10:9; 17:16; 21:26; 40:13; Pss. 22:29; 72:9; 104:29; Prov. 8:26; Isa. 26:5, 19; 40:12; 41:2; 49:23; and Mic. 7:17.

[10] For further study, see Irene Nowell, "Women of Courage and Strength," in *Women in the Old Testament* (Collegeville, Minn.: Liturgical Press, 1997), 153–78.

[11] Alice Ogden Bellis, *Helpmates, Harlots, and Heroes* (Louisville: Westminster/John Knox Press, 1994), 222.

[12] For further study on the book of Judith, see Amy-Jill Levine, "Sacrifice and Salvation: Otherness and Domestication in the Book of Judith," in *A Feminist Companion to Esther, Judith, and Susanna*, ed. Athalya Brenner (Sheffield: Sheffield Academic Press, 1995), 208–23.

[13] See, e.g., Isa. 14:1–2; 17:3–6; 19:24–25; 22:1–25. The focus remains on the countries other than Israel.

[14] This unnamed king of Babylon could be either Nebuchadnezzar, under whom the fall of Judah occurred, or Nabonides, Babylon's last king. It could also be a literary construct that symbolizes any or all of Babylon's wicked kings.

[15] Cf. Ex. 34:6–7, especially verse 7 and, later, Jn. 9:1–3.

[16] The identity of the Assyrian oppressor remains obscure. Possible suggestions include Tiglath-Pileser III, Sargon II, Shalmaneser III, and Sennacherib.

[17] John N. Oswalt, *The Book of Isaiah: Chapters 1—39*, NICOT (Grand Rapids: Eerdmans, 1986), 336.

[18] Christopher R. Seitz, *Isaiah 1—39*, Interpretation (Louisville: John Knox Press, 1993), 139. Walter Brueggemann argues that verses 4b–5 are part of Judah's response to Moab and not part of Moab's plea to Judah. See Brueggemann, *Isaiah 1—39*, WBC (Louisville: Westminster John Knox Press, 1998), 142.

[19] Joseph Jensen, O.S.B., *Isaiah 1—39*, OTM 8 (Wilmington, Del.: Michael Glazier, 1984), 158.

[20] Brueggemann, *Isaiah 1—39*, 145.

[21] J. Alec Motyer, *The Prophecy of Isaiah: An Introduction and Commentary* (Downers Grove, Ill.: InterVarsity, 1993), 156.

[22] For further discussion on the historical outcome of Damascus' existence, see Jensen, *Isaiah 1—39*, 159–60.

[23] Brueggemann, *Isaiah 1—39*, 157.

[24] Marvin A. Sweeney, *Isaiah 1—39 with an Introduction to Prophetic Literature*, FOTL (Grand Rapids: Eerdmans, 1996), 285.

[25] See ibid.

[26] See, e.g., the stories about Anna (Lk. 2:36–38) and the widow who put two copper coins in the temple treasury (Lk. 21:1–4).

[27] Torah obligated the Jewish people to care for certain social classes that were considered endemically vulnerable—namely, the poor, the widows, the fatherless, and the resident aliens (sojourners). See Deut. 10:18, 14, 29; 16:11, 14; 24:19–21; 26:12–13. Failure to do so would result in being cursed by God; see Deut. 27:19.

Chapter 2: Hospitality of Heart

[1] *Des heiligen Ephraem des Syrers Hymnen de paradiso und Contra Julianum*, ed. and trans. Edmond Beck, CSCO (Lourain: Secretariat du Corpus SCO, 1957), 174–75; English translation (with commentary on Genesis, section 2), Sebastion P. Brock, *Hymns on Paradise* (Crestwood, N.Y.: St. Vladimir's Seminary Press, 1990). Also see Carol J. Dempsey, "Hope Amidst Crisis: A Prophetic Vision of Cosmic Redemption," in *All Creation Is Groaning: An Interdisciplinary Vision for Life in a Sacred Universe*, ed. Carol J. Dempsey and Russell A. Butkus (Collegeville, Minn.: Liturgical Press, 1999), 281, where the author first used

this quote in the context of a discussion on Israel's prophets and ethical praxis. See also Dempsey, *Hope Amid the Ruins: The Ethics of Israel's Prophets* (St. Louis: Chalice Press, 2000), 128–29.

²See Isa. 65:17–25.

³Bruce C. Birch, Walter Brueggemann, Terence E. Fretheim, and David L. Petersen, *A Theological Introduction to the Old Testament* (Nashville: Abingdon Press, 1999), 46.

⁴For further discussion on "earth" (*eres*) as "ground," see Dempsey, *Hope Amid the Ruins*, 76, note 54.

⁵As I mention in note 8, p. 24, of *Hope Amid the Ruins*, there are many interpretations of 2:21–23. I especially recognize the recent feminist views on these verses, many of which I affirm. My point here, however, is to underscore creation's diversity.

⁶Birch, Brueggemann, Fretheim, and Petersen, *A Theological Introduction to the Old Testament*, 50. The first part of the divine command given to the human beings is, "Be fruitful and multiply, and fill the earth and subdue it." The word for "subdue" in Hebrew means "to tame," "to bring into bondage." In the context of ancient Israelite monarchal times when this narrative was first "recorded," "subdue" may have meant "to bring under control" or "to have control over" as the point of power a king exercised "over" a people and a country. However, if read in the context of the narrative itself in its narrative setting, which is primordial times, "subdue" could suggest the idea of pruning. Birch *et al* argue that "the verb *subdue*, while capable of more negative senses, here has reference to the earth and its cultivation and, more generally, to the becoming world that is a dynamic, not a static reality," 50.

⁷James Luther Mays, *Psalms,* Interpretation (Louisville: John Knox Press, 1994), 334.

⁸One marvelous story that speaks of hospitality of heart as a motivating principle for justice is the book of Ruth. This narrative describes one woman's great love for another woman after tragedy has struck them both. It also portrays the intricacies of the levirate marriage law and the justice that was extended to Ruth directly and Naomi indirectly, a justice that began with Boaz's kindness of heart.

⁹Scholars differ on the interpretation of "the least of these" in this passage (see vv. 40, 45). The phrase could refer to Christian missionaries who traveled with neither money nor possessions, or it could refer to the poor and needy. For further discussion, see Craig S. Keener, *A Commentary on the Gospel of Matthew* (Grand Rapids: Eerdmans, 1999), 285; John P. Meier, *The Vision of Matthew: Christ, Church, and Morality in the First Gospel* (New York: Crossroad, 1991), 177–78.

¹⁰Jeffrey G. Sobosan, *Bless the Beasts: A Spirituality of Animal Care* (New York: Crossroad, 1991), 23. See also Carol J. Dempsey, "Hope Amidst Crisis," in *All Creation Is Groaning*, 280, where the author first quotes this material from Sobosan.

¹¹Joel B. Green, *The Gospel of Luke* (Grand Rapids: Eerdmans, 1997), 550.

¹²Ibid.

¹³Sharon H. Ringe, *Luke,* WBC (Louisville: Westminster John Knox Press, 1995), 196.

¹⁴Ibid.

¹⁵See Thomas G. Long, *Matthew* (Louisville: Westminster John Knox Press, 1997), 64.

¹⁶Ibid.

¹⁷For further discussion, see Joseph A. Fitzmyer, S.J., *Romans,* AB 33 (New York: Doubleday, 1993), 687–88.

¹⁸Cf. Isa. 11:3; 58:9b; Mt. 7:1–5; Lk. 6:37–38; Jn. 8:15–16.

[19] F. F. Bruce, *The Epistle to the Hebrews,* revised ed. (Grand Rapids: Eerdmans, 1990), 370.

[20] The identities of both Gaius and the writer (who refers to himself as "the elder") remain obscure in biblical scholarship.

Chapter 3: Women, Children, Slaves, and Donkeys

[1] In verse 2, the phrase, "and offer him there as a burnt offering...," reflects ancient cultic practices of worship. Gordan J. Wenham comments on ancient sacrificial practices: "A burnt offering involves cutting up and burning the whole animal on the altar and was the commonest type of sacrifice. It seems to have expressed at least two ideas: that the offerer is giving himself entirely to God (for the animal represents the offerer) and that the animal's death atones for the worshiper's sin. The usual victims of burnt offerings were birds, sheep, or, if the worshiper was very wealthy, a bull. But to offer one's child was quite out of the question for devout orthodox worshipers." See Wenham, *Genesis 16—50,* WBC 2 (Dallas: Word Books, 1994), 105.

[2] For further discussion on the understanding of "fear" as awe and great love, see the discussion on "fear of the Lord" by Alexander A. DiLella in Patrick W. Skehan and Alexander DiLella, *Wisdom of Ben Sirach,* AB 39 (New York: Doubleday, 1987), 75–76.

[3] See, e.g., the call of Moses, the divine command associated with his call, and his verbal reluctance (Ex. 3:1–12); cf. Jeremiah's call narrative and mission (Jer. 1:4–10).

[4] Genesis 22:1–19 enjoys a long history of interpretation, of which I am well aware. Given the focus of this volume on biblical justice, I am offering a rereading of the Abraham-Isaac story in light of the Prophets, and in light of the New Testament portrayal of Jesus, whose writers seem to understand him in relation to the tradition of Abraham, Isaac, David, and Solomon (see, e.g., Mt. 1:1–17), and as one who embodies the tradition of the Prophets. (See, e.g., Mt. 12:15–21; Mk. 12:1–12; Lk. 4:16–30; Jn. 8:39—59.)

[5] The other stories include 2 Kings 4:8–37, 4:38–41, and 4:42–44. For additional discussion on 2 Kings 4 as "miracle stories," see Terence E. Fretheim, *First and Second Kings* (Louisville: Westminster John Knox Press, 1999), 146.

[6] Ibid., 146–47.

[7] Ibid.

[8] Claudia V. Camp, "1 and 2 Kings," in *Women's Bible Commentary,* expanded edition with Apocrypha, ed. Carol A. Newsom and Sharon H. Ringe (Louisville: Westminster John Knox Press, 1998), 113.

[9] Tolbert, "Mark," in *Women's Bible Commentary,* 355.

[10] Ibid.

[11] Joel B. Green, *The Gospel of Luke* (Grand Rapids: Eerdmans, 1997), xxx.

[12] Ibid.

[13] Ibid.

[14] Ibid.

[15] John Gerald Janzen, *Exodus,* WBC (Louisville: Westminster John Knox Press, 1997), 162.

[16] J. Phillip Hyatt, *Exodus,* NCBC (Grand Rapids: Eerdmans, 1980), 228.

[17] For further discussion, see Janzen, *Exodus.*

[18] Hyatt, *Exodus,* p. 229.

[19] Janzen, *Exodus,* p. 162.

[20] Hyatt, *Exodus,* 228.

[21] Ibid., 234.

[22] Terence E. Fretheim, *Exodus,* Interpretation (Louisville: John Knox Press, 1991), 249.

Notes for Pages 82–104

[23] The sequence of events between verses 20–21 and verse 22 are inconsistent because of two different traditions. Verse 20 belongs to E; verses 21–35 belong to J.
[24] For further study on this passage, see Baruch A. Levine, *Numbers 21-36*, AB 4A (New York: Doubleday, 2000), 137–59.
[25] Brian Patrick, as quoted in Michael Dowd, *Earthspirit: A Handbook for Nurturing an Ecological Christianity* (Mystic, Conn.: Twenty-Third Pub., 1991), 54.

Chapter 4: Compassion

[1] Meister Eckhart, as quoted in Matthew Fox, *Meditations with Meister Eckhart* (Santa Fe: Bear & Company, Inc., 1982), 111.
[2] Ibid., 110.
[3] Wayne Teasdale, *The Mystic Heart* (New York: New World Library, 2001), 76.
[4] Joan Chittister, *The Illuminated Life: Monastic Wisdom for Seekers of Light* (New York: Orbis Books, 2001), 114–15.
[5] Eckhart, as quoted in Fox, *Meditations with Meister Eckhart*, 103.
[6] Cf. Gen. 3:7.
[7] To be noted is that, according to the biblical text, only the man is described as being cast out of the garden; see verse 24.
[8] Recall the discussion early in the book about evaluating divine justice in the Bible.
[9] Admah and Zeboiim are two cities usually mentioned with Sodom and Gomorrah. All four cities were noted for their wickedness, and they shared the same fate—devastation. In Hos. 11:8 they serve to highlight how terrible God's wrath can be.
[10] Cf. Jas. 2:1—13, which speaks of mercy triumphing over judgment.
[11] Cf. Mt. 22:34–40.
[12] See, e.g., 1 QS, the Manual of Discipline of the Essene Community,. 1:8ff; Lk. 5:1–4.
[13] See Mt. 14:14; 15:32; 18:27; 20:34; cf. Phil. 2:1.
[14] Cf. Rom. 13:8–10 and Gal. 5:13–15. The antithesis of love for one's neighbor is the story of the rich man and Lazarus (Lk. 16:19–31). For further comment on "right relationship," see Gregory J. Polan, O.S.B., "Justice," in *The Collegeville Pastoral Dictionary of Biblical Theology*, ed. Carroll Stuhlmueller (Collegeville, Minn.: The Liturgical Press, 1996), 510.
[15] For further study on God as relational, see Elizabeth A. Johnson, *She Who Is: The Mystery of God in Feminist Theological Discourse* (New York: Crossroad, 1992), especially 191–223 and the chapter "Suffering God: Compassion Poured Out," 246–72.
[16] Cf. Ps. 89:14.

Chapter 5: Peace

[1] For further discussion, see Carol J. Dempsey, "Torah: An Attitude and Way of Life That Inform the Ethics of Israel's Prophets," *Hope Amid the Ruins: The Ethics of Israel's Prophets* (St. Louis: Chalice Press, 2000), 35–45.
[2] For further comment, see Carol J. Dempsey, *The Prophets: A Liberation-Critical Reading* (Minneapolis: Fortress Press, 2000), 164–65.
[3] This passage is part of a collection that has been traditionally known as the Servant Songs (Isa. 42:1–4; 49:1–6; 50:4–9; and 52:13—53:12). There is no consensus about the identity of the servant, and arguments have been made that it could be the prophet himself or one from the Isaian School, or Israel, or

a literary construct that remains a vision and a picture of hope for all people to embrace.

[4]See also Isa. 49:1–7, which describes Israel as God's servant through whom God will accomplish the divine plan of universal salvation.

[5]See John J. Collins, "Isaiah," in *Collegeville Bible Commentary*, ed. Dianne Bergant (Collegeville, Minn.: The Liturgical Press, 1992), 449.

[6]Verse 2b juxtaposes a year of divine favor with a "day" of divine vengeance. On the one hand, this verse can be troubling; on the other, it suggests a gradual movement toward a new world order, which does not come to fulfillment until a later time. The transformation into the peaceable kingdom—the time of jubilee—is an evolving process and not an instant event. The verse points forward to Lk. 4:18–19, which describes Jesus' self-understanding of his mission in relation to Isa. 61:1–2. The "day of vengeance of our God" is absent in the Lukan text and the Isaian scroll from which Jesus reads.

[7]For additional comment on justice to the Gentiles, see further the writings of Paul—especially Romans, Galatians, and other passages in Ephesians.

[8]Rabbi Rami M. Shapiro, as quoted in Elizabeth Roberts and Elias Amidon, eds., *Earth Prayers* (San Francisco: Harper San Francisco, 1991), 112.

Epilogue

[1]James Irwin, cited in Michael Reagan, *The Hand of God: Thoughts and Images Reflecting the Spirit of the Universe* (Philadelphia: Templeton Foundation Press, 1999), 158.

Select Bibliography

Beck, Edmond, ed. *Des heiligen Ephraem des Syrers Hymnen de paradiso und Contra Julianum.* Edited and translated by Edmond Beck, CSCO, 174–75. Lourain: Secretariat du Corpus SCO, 1957. English translation (with commentary on Genesis, section 2), *Hymns on Paradise.* Translated by Sebastion P. Brock. Crestwood, N.Y.: St. Vladimir's Seminary Press, 1990.

Bellis, Alice Ogden. *Helpmates, Harlots, and Heroes.* Louisville: Westminster/John Knox Press, 1994.

Birch, Bruce C., Walter Brueggemann, Terence E. Fretheim, and David L. Petersen, *A Theological Introduction to the Old Testament.* Nashville: Abingdon Press, 1999.

Bruce, F.F. *The Epistle to the Hebrews,* revised ed. Grand Rapids: Eerdmans, 1990.

Brueggemann, Walter. *Isaiah 1—39.* WBC. Louisville: Westminster John Knox Press, 1998.

Chittister, Joan. *The Illuminated Life: Monastic Wisdom for Seekers of Light.* New York: Orbis Books, 2001.

Dempsey, Carol J., and Russell A. Butkus, eds. *All Creation Is Groaning: An Interdisciplinary Vision for Life in a Sacred Universe.* Collegeville: The Liturgical Press, 1999.

Dempsey, Carol J. *Hope Amid the Ruins: The Ethics of Israel's Prophets.* St. Louis: Chalice Press, 2000.

____. *Jeremiah: Preacher of Grace, Poet of Truth.* Collegeville, Minn.: The Liturgical Press, 2007.

____. "Plagues," in *Pastoral Dictionary of Biblical Theology.* Edited by Dianne Bergant, CSA; Leslie Hoppe, OFM; and Barbara Reid, OP. General editor, Carroll Stuhlmueller, CP. Collegeville, Minn.: Liturgical Press, 1996, 739–41.

____. *The Prophets: A Liberation-Critical Reading.* Minneapolis: Fortress Press, 2000.

Dowd, Michael. *Earthspirit: A Handbook for Nurturing an Ecological Christianity.* Mystic, Conn.: Twenty-Third Pub., 1991.

Fitzmyer, Joseph A., S.J. *Romans.* AB 33. New York: Doubleday, 1993.

Fretheim, Terence E. *Exodus.* Interpretation Series. Louisville: John Knox Press, 1991.

____. *First and Second Kings.* WBC; Louisville: Westminster John Knox Press, 1999).

Fox, Matthew. *Meditations with Meister Eckhart.* Santa Fe: Bear & Company, Inc., 1982.

Green, Joel B. *The Gospel of Luke.* Grand Rapids: Eerdmans, 1997.

Hyatt, Philip. *Exodus.* New Century Bible Commentary. Grand Rapids: Eerdmans, 1980.

Jensen, Joseph, O.S.B. *Isaiah 1—39.* OTM 8. Wilmington, Del.: Michael Glazier, 1984.

Johnson, Elizabeth. *She Who Is: The Mystery of God in Feminist Theological Discourse.* New York: Crossroad, 1992.

Keener, Craig. *A Commentary on the Gospel of Matthew.* Grand Rapids: Eerdmans, 1999.

Larsson, Göran. *Bound for Freedom: The Book of Exodus in Jewish and Christian Traditions.* Peabody: Hendrickson, 1999.

Leclerc, Thomas L. *Yahweh Is Exalted in Justice: Solidarity and Conflict in Isaiah.* Minneapolis: Fortress Press, 2001.

Levine, Amy-Jill. "Sacrifice and Salvation: Otherness and Domestication in the Book of Judith," in *A Feminist Companion to Esther, Judith, and Susanna.* Edited by Athalya Brenner. Sheffield: Sheffield Academic Press, 1995, pp. 208–23.

Levine, Baruch A. *Numbers 21—36.* AB 4A. New York: Doubleday, 2000.

Long, Thomas G. *Matthew.* Louisville: Westminster John Knox Press, 1997.

Meier, John P. *The Vision of Matthew: Christ, Church, and Morality in the First Gospel.* New York: Crossroad, 1991.

Motyer, J. Alec. *The Prophecy of Isaiah: An Introduction and Commentary.* Downers Grove, Ill.: InterVarsity Press, 1993.

Nardoni, Enrique. *Rise Up, O Judge: A Study of Justice in the Biblical World.*. Translated by Sean Charles Martin. Peabody, Mass.: Hendrickson, 2004.

Newsom, Carol A., and Sharon H. Ringe, eds. *Women's Bible Commentary*, expanded ed. with Apocrypha. Louisville: Westminster John Knox Press, 1998.

Nowell, Irene. "Women of Courage and Strength," in *Women in the Old Testament.* Collegeville, Minn.: The Liturgical Press, 1997, 153–78.

Oswalt, John N. *The Book of Isaiah: Chapters 1—39*. NICOT. Grand Rapids: Eerdmans, 1986.

Polan, Gregory J., O.S.B. "Justice," in *The Collegeville Pastoral Dictionary of Biblical Theology.* Edited by Carroll Stuhlmueller. Collegeville, Minn.: The Liturgical Press, 1996.

Reagan, Michael. *The Hand of God: Thoughts and Images Reflecting the Spirit of the Universe.* Philadelphia: Templeton Foundation Press, 1999.

Ringe, Sharon H. *Luke.* WBC. Louisville: Westminster John Knox Press, 1995.

Roberts, Elizabeth and Elias Amidon, eds. *Earth Prayers.* San Francisco: Harper San Francisco, 1991.

Seitz, Christopher R. *Isaiah 1—39.* Interpretation Series. Louisville: John Knox Press, 1993.

Skehan, Patrick S., and Alexander A. DiLella. *Wisdom of Ben Sirach.* AB 39. New York: Doubleday, 1987.

Sobosan, Jeffrey. *Bless the Beasts: A Spirituality of Animal Care.* New York: Crossroad, 1991.

Sweeney, Marvin A. *Isaiah 1—39 with an Introduction to Prophetic Literature.* FOTL. Grand Rapids: Eerdmans, 1996.

Teasdale, Wayne. *The Mystic Heart.* New York: New World Library, 2001.

Wenham, Gordon J. *Genesis 16—50.* WBC 2. Dallas: Word Books, 1994.

Biblical Index

Genesis

1—2	46–48, 50
1—11	88
1:1–2	108
1:1—2:4a	47
1:10	47
1:12	47
1:18	47
1:21	47
1:22	48
1:25	47
1:26	50, 84, 98
1:26–27	94
1:27	48
1:28	48–49, 89
1:31	47
2:4b–5	48
2:4b–25	47
2:7	47, 108
2:9	47
2:15	48
2:18–20	48
2:19	47
2:21–23	117
3—11	11
3:1–7	89
3:1–12	118
3:1–24	83, 88–89
3:7	119
3:8–13	89
3:14–19	89
3:19	115
3:20–21	89
3:21	89
3:22–24	89
4:1	89
4:1–16	11–12, 42, 90
4:1–17	36
4:8	11, 90
4:9–15	90
4:9a	11, 90
4:9b	11, 90
4:10	90
4:10–12	11
4:11–12	90
4:13–16	11
4:14	90
16:4–5	65
17:12	79
17:27	79
18:1–8	60
18:19	115
21:8	64
21:8–12	64
21:8–21	66
21:9	65
21:9–10	64
21:9–14	64
21:10	65
21:11	64
21:12	65
21:12–13	64
21:14	64
21:15–16	65, 66
21:15–19	64
21:16	65
21:17	65
21:17a	65
21:17–18	66
21:19	65
21:20	66
21:20–21	65
22:1b–8	67
22:1–19	66, 118
22:2	118
22:6	68
22:7	68
22:9	67
22:9–14	67
22:12	67
22:13	67, 69
22:15–18	67
29:31	89

Exodus

1:8–14	70
1:8–22	70
1:8—2:10	69, 71
1:8—7:13	13
1:15–22	70
2:1–3	71
2:1–10	70
2:4	71
2:5–10	71
2:23–25	38
7:14–25	14
7:14—12:42	13
7:21	14
7:23	14–15
7:24	14–15
8:1–15	14
8:16–19	14
8:17	14
8:18	14
8:19	14
8:20–32	15
8:24	15
9:1–7	15
9:2	15
9:3	15
9:4	15
9:6	15
9:8–12	15
9:9	15
9:11	15
9:13	15
9:13–35	15
9:14	15
9:16	15
9:20–21	15
9:25	16
9:26	16
9:33–34	16
9:35	16
10:1–20	16
10:15	16
10:20	16
10:21–29	16
10:23	16
10:27	16
11:1–10	16
11:5–7	17
12:29	17
12:29–32	16
21:1–11	78, 81
21:1–32	81
21:2	78
21:2–6	78–79
21:3	78
21:4	78
21:5–6	79
21:6	79
21:7	72
21:7–11	78–80
21:12–25	12
21:20	80
21:20–21	78, 80–81
21:21–23	97
21:23–25	115
21:26–27	78, 80–81
34:6–7	12, 116
34:7	116

Leviticus

15:25–30	73
19:18	57, 85, 94
20:10	93
22:11	79
24:19–21	115
25:1–7	104
25:8–55	104
25:18–19	101

Numbers

21:24–30	27
22:20	119
22:20–21	119
22:21–35	119
22:22	82, 119
22:22–23	82
22:22–35	64, 82–83
22:23	82
22:24	82
22:25	82
22:26	82
22:27	82
22:28	83–84
22:28–30	82
22:30a	83
22:30b	84
22:31–35	83
22:34	84
32:1–5	27
33—38	27

Biblical Index 127

Deuteronomy
6:1–9	12
6:4–6	106
6:5	94
7:7–8	45
7:7–11	91, 115
10:12ff	85
10:12–16	106
10:12–20	12
10:16	45
10:18	116
10:19	95
14:28–29	85
14:29	116
15:1–8	104
15:12	72
15:17	79
16:11	116
16:14	116
16:20	115
19:21	115
24:19–21	116
24:17	85, 115
25:5–10	97
26:12–13	116
27:19	116
28	9

Judges
3:12–30	27
11:22–26	27

1 Samuel
1:5–6	89
14:47	27

1 Kings
10:9	115

2 Kings
3:4–27	27
4	71
4:1	77
4:1–7	71
4:8–37	118
4:38–41	118
4:42–44	118

Nehemiah
5:1–5	77

Judith
8	20
9	20
9—16	19
9:2–6	20
9:7–10	20
9:14	20
10	20
10:1–10	20
10:11–23	20
11—12	20
12:13–16	20
12:17–20	20
13	20–21
13:2	20
13:4	21
13:5	21
13:6–8	21
13:8–10	21
14—15	21
16	19, 21
16:17	21
16:21–25	21

Job
4:19	115
10:9	115
17:16	115
21:26	115
21:26	115
40:13	115

Psalms
8	50
22:29	115
72:8–14	49
72:9	115
89:14	119
104	50, 61
104:1–30	49
104:10–23	49
104:14–15	50
104:14–15a	50
104:23	50
104:24	49
104:24c	49
104:27–30	50
104:29	115
145:8–9	93, 99
145:17	99

Proverbs

8:26	115

Ecclesiastes

3:20	115

Wisdom of Solomon

11:24–26	82
12:1	98, 108

Sirach

18:13	82

Isaiah

1:16–17	115
1:17	115
2:1–4	104
2:2–4	5, 18, 34, 102, 115
5:8–13	115
7:8	29
9:1–7	102
9:7	104
11:1	103
11:1–3	103, 108
11:1–9	103
11:2	103–4
11:3	117
11:3a	103
11:3b–5	103
11:6	103
11:7	103
13—23	23, 31, 34, 103
13:1	23
13:1–22	23, 25
13:2–3	24
13:3	24
13:4c	24
13:6	24
13:6–12	25
13:9	24
13:11	24
13:14–18	24
13:16a	25
13:16b	25
13:17	24
13:17–19	25
13:18	25
13:19–22	24
14:1	26
14:1–2	116
14:3–23	23–24
14:13–14	25
14:20	25
14:20b–21	26
14:21–23	25
14:24–27	23, 26
14:25	26
14:28–32	23, 26
14:30	27
14:31	27
15:1—16:11	28
15:1—16:14	23, 27–28
15:1–9	27
15:4b–5	116
15:12	28
15:13	28
16:1–5	27
16:6–7	28
16:6–12	28
16:8–12	28
16:12–13	28
16:14	28
17:1–3	23, 29
17:3–6	116
18:1–2	29
18:1–7	23, 29
18:2	29
18:3–6	29
18:7	29–30
19:1	30
19:1–17	23, 30–31
19:2	30
19:3	30
19:4	30–31
19:5–7	31
19:16	31
19:17	31
19:24–25	116
10:11–15	31
21:1–10	23, 25, 32
21:9b	25
21:11–12	23, 31
21:13	32
21:13–17	23, 32
21:13b–15	32
21:14	32
21:16–17	32
21:14	32
21:17	32

Biblical Index 129

22:1–25	116	5:1–6	34
23:1–14	33	5:6	34
23:1–18	23, 32–33	5:6–7	34
23:9	33	5:7	35
23:11	33	5:9	35
23:11a	33	5:12	34
23:11b	33	5:13	34
23:13	33	5:14–17	34
23:14	33	5:14a	34
23:15	33	5:15–17	34
23:15–18	33	5:18	35
23:17	33	5:18–19	35
23:18	33	5:19	35
26:5	115	5:20–31	35
26:19	115	5:28	35
32:14–15	102	5:29	35
32:16–17	102	5:30–31	34
40:12	115	21:12	115
41:2	115	22:3	115
42:1	104	31:31–34	105
42:1a	103	31:33	45
42:1b	103	46—51	103
42:1–4	43, 103, 105, 108, 115, 119	46:1—56:58	118
		50:13	11
49:1–6	119	50:17–18	11
49:1–7	120		
49:23	115	**Ezekiel**	
50:4–9	119	3:27	84
52:13—53:12	119	25:1—32:32	115
55:7	115	33:17–20	115
56:1	115	33:22	84
56:1–8	106	34:1–4	49
58:6	38	36:1–7	115
58:6–14	69	36:26	45
58:9b	117		
59:9–15	2	**Hosea**	
61:1–2	105, 120	2:16–20	102
61:1–4	103–4	4:1–3	115
61:2b	120	4:1–10	115
65:17	61	6:1	115
65:17–25	43, 117	6:1–3	105
		9:14	89
Jeremiah		11:1–2	91
1:4–10	118	11:1–9	91
2:14	79	11:3–4	91
3:12	115	11:5–7	92
3:14	115	11:8	123
3:22	115	11:8–9	36, 42, 92, 115
4:4	45	11:9	12
5	34–36	14:1	115

Amos

1:2—2:3	115
1:3–5	29
2:6	77
7:7–9	29

Micah

2:1–2	115
2:1–3	10
2:8–9	115
3:1–12	115
3:8	108
4:1–5	18, 102–3, 115
6:6–7	3
6:6–8	105
6:8	3, 112
7:1–6	115
7:8–10	91
7:17	115
7:18–20	12, 36, 90–91, 115

Nahum

1:2–3	12

Zephaniah

1:2–6	12
2:9	27
2:10	27

Malachi

3:7	115

Matthew

1:1–17	118
1:8ff	119
5—7	94
5:43	57
5:44	57
5:44–45	115
5:45	57
5:46–47	57
5:48	58
5:25	94
6:25–34	94
6:26	94
6:30	94
7:1–5	117
9:35–38	96
11:28–30	45
12:15–21	104, 118
12:18	106, 115
12:18–21	108
12:20	115
12:21	106
12:18–21	4, 43
14:13–21	96
14:14	96, 119
15:32	97, 119
15:32–39	96–97
15:33–39	97
18:27	119
20:34	119
22:34–40	12, 104, 119
23:1–3	39
23:1–36	37–38, 104
23:4–7	39
23:8–10	39
23:11–12	39
23:13–36	39
23:23	4, 39, 115
23:26	104
24:3—25:46	51
24:3	51
24:31–33	51–52
24:34–36	52
24:34–46	51
24:37–39	52
24:40	52
24:41	52
24:46	52
25:31–46	51–52
25:34	54
25:40	51, 117
25:45	117

Mark

5:21–43	73
5:22–23	73
5:24	73
5:25–28	73
5:26	73
5:34	74
5:37–43	74
9:14–29	74
9:18	74
9:22	74–75
9:23	75

9:24	75	18:1	37
9:28–29	75	18:1–8	37, 98
12:1–12	118	18:2	37
		18:3	37
Luke		18:4	37
1:76–79	113	18:5	37
2:29–32	106	18:6–8a	38
2:34	40	18:15–17	75
2:34–35	40	18:15	75
2:36–38	116	18:16–17	76
4:16–19	108	18:18	76
4:16–30	104, 118	18:31–34	40
4:17–19	104	18:34a	40
4:18–19	120	19:42	109
4:19	105	21:1–4	116
4:21	105	22:34–40	106
4:24	40	22:34a	42
4:31–37	105	22:39–43	41
5:1–4	119	22:43	41
5:12–16	105	22:47–53	40
5:17–26	105	22:54–62	40
6:1–5	105	22:63–65	40
6:27–31	12	22:66—23:12	40
6:37–38	117	23:26–42	37
7:1–10	105	23:26–43	4, 40
7:11–17	97, 105	23:34	4, 12, 105
7:13	97		
7:14–15	97	**John**	
7:16–17	98	7:53—8:11	92
7:44–46	76	8:10	93
8:26–39	105	8:11	93
9:21–27	40	8:15–16	117
9:43–45	40	8:39–59	118
10:6	106	9:1–3	116
10:25–37	94, 96, 105		
10:27	96	**Acts**	
10:29	95	2:17–18	108
10:31–32	95	10:34–43	106
11:37–53	105	10:44–48	106
11:42	115	11:1–18	106
11:49–52	40	13:44–52	106
14:1	54	15:14	106
14:7–11	54		
14:7–14	54	**Philippians**	
14:8–11	54	1:7	46
14:11	54	2:1	119
14:12–14	54–56		
15:21–28	106	**2 Corinthians**	
16:19–31	119	1:22	46
17:20–21	104	11—13	46

Philemon

1:8	59–60
1:17	60

Hebrews

13:1	59
13:1–2	59–60
13:2	60
13:1–19	59

Ephesians

2	107
2:11–22	107
2:14	108
3:6	106
3:17	46

Galatians

5:13–15	119

Romans

11:11–24	106
11:13	106
13:8–10	119
14:1–12	58–59
14:1—15:13	58
14:1	58
14:4	58
14:5–6	58
14:7–8	59
14:7–12	59
14:10	59
14:12	59
15:7	58

Colossians

1:15–20	105
3:12–15	99

3 John

1:2–8	59–60

James

2:1–13	119

Index of Authors and Terms

A

Abraham 60, 64–69, 91, 118
Adam 88–89, 93
Amidon, Elias 120
anawim 57
animals 7, 14–18, 24, 29, 46–50, 53, 69, 82–84, 101–2
apostasy 34
Assyria 11, 19, 23, 26, 29, 101
Assyrians 19–22, 26–27, 30, 116

B

Babylon 11, 23–25, 32–33, 63, 104, 116
Babylonians 19, 23–25, 63
Balaam 64, 82–84
Beck, Edmond, CSCO 116
Bellis, Alice Ogden 21, 116
Bergant, Dianne 115, 120
Birch, Bruce C. 49, 117
birds 29, 46, 48–49, 94, 102, 118
Brenner, Athalya 116
Brock, Sebastian P. 116
Bruce, F. F. 60, 118
Brueggemann, Walter 30, 49, 116, 117
Butkus, Russell A. 116

C

Cain 11–12, 89–90, 93, 98
Camp, Claudia V. 72, 118
children vii, 7–8, 24–25, 63–64, 71–78, 84, 89, 118
Chittister, Joan 88, 119
Collins, John J. 104, 120

commandments 12, 107
compassion 4, 6–7, 11, 36, 40–42, 46, 58, 64, 69, 71, 82, 85, 87–99, 105, 112, 119
creation ii, 5–8, 25, 38, 40, 46–50, 53, 61, 82, 88, 93–94, 98–99, 103, 108, 111–12, 116–17

D

Damascus 23, 29, 116
Dempsey, Carol 115–17
deuteronomic theology of love 12
deuteronomistic theology of retribution 5, 9–10, 12, 34, 42
DiLella, Alexander A. 118
dominion 6, 49–51, 61, 93–94
donkey 15, 64, 82–84, 118
Dowd, Michael 119
Dumah 23, 31–32

E

Eckhart, Meister 87–88, 119
Egypt 13–17, 23, 30–31, 63, 65, 70, 115
Egyptians 13–16, 18, 30–31, 64–65, 69–70, 91, 115
Elisha 71–72
Ephraem of Syria 46, 116
Ethiopia 23, 29–30
Ethiopians 29–30
Eve 88–89, 93

F

Fitzmyer, Joseph A., SJ 117
flesh 21, 45, 61, 107–8
forgiveness 40–42, 91, 105, 113

Fox, Matthew 119
Fretheim, Terence E. 49, 72, 81, 117–18

G

Gentile(s) 4, 58, 60, 106–7, 120
good life 60, 101
Green, Joel B. 54–55, 76, 117–18

H

Hagar 64–66
heart(s) 2–3, 6, 8, 13–18, 30, 33, 36, 39, 42–43, 45–47, 49–53, 57–61, 71, 73, 85, 87–88, 91–92, 95–96, 98–99, 105, 107, 112, 116–17, 119
Holofernes 19–22, 42
hospitality 6, 46, 51–52, 54–61, 76–77, 98, 107, 116–17
Hyatt, J. Phillip 77, 79, 81, 115, 118
hypocrisy 39

I

idolatry 34
inheritance 10, 51, 97, 104
injustice 2–4, 8, 10–11, 17–19, 22–23, 33, 36, 38, 40–41, 46, 51, 53, 57, 61, 63, 69, 81, 83, 91–92, 112
intrinsic goodness 6, 42, 46–47, 50–51, 61
Irwin, James 111, 120
Isaac 64–69, 118
Ishmael 64–67
Israel 2–4, 6, 10–11, 13–15, 17–20, 23, 25–29, 36, 42, 68, 77, 90–92, 101–2, 106–7, 115–20
Israelites 2–3, 5, 9–10, 13–22, 42, 45, 70, 77–78, 80, 91, 117

J

Jairus 73–74
Janzen, John Gerald 77, 79, 118
Jensen, Joseph, OSB 116
Johnson, Elizabeth A. 119

Judah 19, 23, 26–28, 31, 34–35, 116
Judahites 31, 34–35, 104
Judas 40
judgment 16, 21, 23–25, 30, 34–35, 51, 58–59, 77, 91, 119
Judith 12, 19–23, 42, 116
justice ii, vii, 1–43, 45–46, 51–54, 56–61, 63–64, 66–68, 70–78, 80–82, 84–85, 87–90, 92–94, 96–98, 101–6, 108, 111–12, 115–20

K

Kedar 32
Keener, Craig S. 117

L

lamentation 28, 33
land(s) 6, 13–18, 24–27, 32, 35, 63, 65, 69, 82, 101–4
Larsson, Goran 115
law(s) 4, 6,9, 12, 39, 45, 57–58, 60–61, 71, 78–79, 80–82, 90, 92, 95, 97–98, 101, 105–7, 112, 115, 117
Leclerc, Thomas L. 115
Levine, Amy–Jill 116
Levine, Baruch A. 119
lex talionis 5, 9–12, 25, 34–35, 42, 115
liberation 7, 9, 13, 17, 22–23, 26–27, 42, 69–70, 75, 80–81, 102, 112, 115, 119
Long, Thomas G. 117
loving-kindness 2–3

M

Mays, James Luther 49, 117
Meier, John P. 117
mission 7, 12, 40, 67, 69, 96, 104–6, 108, 118, 120
Moab 23, 27–28, 82–83, 116
monarchy 6, 20
Moses 13–16, 39, 69–71, 78, 118
Motyer, J. Alec 116

N

Nardoni, Enrique 115
nation 5, 11, 19–21, 23, 25–27, 29–31, 33–35, 42–43, 51, 66, 91, 102–3, 109, 115
Nebuchadnezzar 11, 19, 116
nonhuman 7–8, 13–14, 18, 42, 46, 48–49, 53, 61, 84, 101, 103, 112
Nowell, Irene 116

O

Oswalt, John N. 27, 116

P

parousia 51
Patrick, Brian 84, 119
peace 5, 7, 23, 38, 74, 99, 101–9, 112–13, 119
penitence 91
Petersen, David L. 49, 117
Philistia 23, 26–27
plagues 13, 15–16, 115
plants 16, 18, 47, 50
Polan, Gregory J., OSB 119
poor 27, 34, 51, 54–57, 72, 84–85, 116–17
power 2, 6–7, 10, 13, 15, 17–18, 20, 23, 25–26, 28–34, 39, 64, 69–70, 73–75, 77, 80, 117

R

Reagan, Michael 120
reconciliation 4, 84, 98, 105, 107
retribution 5–6, 9–10, 34–36, 42
right relationship 2, 7, 61, 84, 88, 93–94, 96–98, 103, 105–6, 108, 112, 119
righteousness 1–2, 7, 28, 53, 59, 95, 102–3
Ringe, Sharon 56–57, 117, 118
Roberts, Michael 120

S

Sabbath 54, 58

salvation 2, 13, 19, 40, 69–71, 104, 106, 113, 115–16, 120
Sarah 64–66
Seitz, Christopher R. 116
Shapiro, Rabbi Rami M. 108, 120
Skehan, Patrick W. 118
slave 6–7, 59–60, 63–65, 76–81, 118
Sobosan, Jeffrey G. 117, 153
Stuhlmueller, Carroll 119
Sweeney, Marvin A. 116
synagogue 73, 96, 105

T

Teasdale, Wayne 87–88, 119
Tolbert, Wayne 73, 118
Torah 12, 38, 45, 57, 85, 101, 109, 116, 119
transgression(s) 2–3, 7, 13, 34–35, 84, 88–93
Tyre 23, 32–33

U

Uzziah 21

V

violence 2, 9, 11, 13, 18, 22–23, 26–27, 31, 33, 35, 42, 46, 53, 81, 84, 104, 112
vision 2, 4–5, 8, 18, 25, 30, 34, 36, 38, 40, 42–43, 46–48, 53, 61, 63, 69, 84–85, 99, 101–4, 108, 112, 116–17, 120
vocation 4, 8, 42–43, 84, 99, 108, 111, 113
vulnerable 2, 25, 37–38, 61, 63, 66, 74, 76–77, 80, 116

W

Wenham, Gordon J. 118
widow(s) 37–38, 71–72, 85, 97–98, 116